# Discretion in the Welfare State

Welfare state professionals decide or establish premises as to whom will receive what, in what manner, when and how much, and when enough is enough. They control who passes through the gates of the welfare state.

This book provides an in-depth understanding of the phenomenon of discretion. It shows why the delegation of discretionary powers to professionals in the front-line of the welfare state is both unavoidable and problematic. Extensive use of discretion can threaten the principles of the rule of law and relinquish democratic control over the implementation of laws and policies. The book introduces an understanding of discretion that adds an epistemic dimension (discretion as a mode of reasoning) to the common structural understanding of discretion (an area of judgment and decision). Accordingly, it distinguishes between structural and epistemic measures of accountability. The aim of the former is to constrain discretionary spaces or the behavior within them while the aim of the latter is to improve the quality of discretionary reasoning.

This text will be of key interest to scholars and students in the fields of applied philosophy, public policy and public administration, welfare state research, and the sociology of professions.

**Anders Molander** is Associate Professor at Centre for the Study of Professions, Oslo and Akershus University College, Norway.

# Routledge Advances in European Politics

*For a complete list of titles in this series, please visit* www.routledge.com/Routledge-Advances-in-European-Politics/book-series/AEP

**122 Eurozone Politics**
Perception and reality in Italy, the UK, and Germany
*Philip Giurlando*

**123 Politics of Identity in Post-Conflict States**
The Bosnian and Irish experience
*Edited by Éamonn Ó Ciardha and Gabriela Vojvoda*

**124 Unequal Europe**
Social divisions and social cohesion in an old continent
*James Wickham*

**125 Clientelism and Economic Policy**
Greece and the Crisis
*Aris Trantidis*

**126 Challenges to Democracies in East-Central Europe**
*Edited by Jan Holzer and Miroslav Mareš*

**127 Iceland's Financial Crisis**
The politics of blame, protest, and reconstruction
*Edited by Valur Ingimundarson, Philippe Urfalino and Irma Erlingsdóttir*

**128 Personal Diplomacy in the EU**
Political Leadership and Critical Junctures of European Integration
*Roland Vogt*

**129 Discretion in the Welfare State**
Social rights and professional judgment
*Anders Molander*

# Discretion in the Welfare State
Social rights and professional judgment

**Anders Molander**

LONDON AND NEW YORK

First published 2016 by Routledge

2 Park Square, Milton Park, Abingdon, Oxfordshire OX14 4RN

711 Third Avenue, New York, NY 10017

*Routledge is an imprint of the Taylor & Francis Group, an informa business*

First issued in paperback 2018

Copyright © 2016 Anders Molander

The right of Anders Molander to be identified as author of this work has been asserted by him in accordance with sections 77 and 78 of the Copyright, Designs and Patents Act 1988.

All rights reserved. No part of this book may be reprinted or reproduced or utilised in any form or by any electronic, mechanical, or other means, now known or hereafter invented, including photocopying and recording, or in any information storage or retrieval system, without permission in writing from the publishers.

Notice:
Product or corporate names may be trademarks or registered trademarks, and are used only for identification and explanation without intent to infringe.

*British Library Cataloguing in Publication Data*
A catalogue record for this book is available from the British Library

*Library of Congress Cataloging-in-Publication Data*
Names: Molander, Anders, author.
Title: Discretion in the welfare state : social rights and professional judgment / Anders Molander.
Description: Abingdon, Oxon ; New York, NY : Routledge, 2017. | Series: Routledge advances in European politics ; 129 | Includes bibliographical references and index.
Identifiers: LCCN 2016025574 | ISBN 9781138212428 (hardback) | ISBN 9781315450483 (ebook)
Subjects: LCSH: Social work administration. | Administrative discretion. | Social service—Decision making. | Welfare state—Decision making. | Social rights.
Classification: LCC HV41 .M525 2017 | DDC 361.0068/4—dc23
LC record available at https://lccn.loc.gov/2016025574

ISBN: 978-1-138-21242-8 (hbk)
ISBN: 978-1-138-32643-9 (pbk)

Typeset in Times New Roman
by Apex CoVantage, LLC

For Harald, my friend and colleague

# Contents

*Preface* viii

Introduction 1

1 Discretion and its critics 7

2 The anatomy of discretion 20

3 Professional discretion in the welfare state: two normative tensions 47

4 Mechanisms of accountability 60

5 Summing up 78

*Bibliography* 80
*Index* 88

# Preface

This little book is the result of a close cooperation with Harald Grimen, my colleague and friend who died unexpectedly owing to a fatal error during heart surgery in February 2011. The basic ideas were first developed while Harald and I were working with Erik Oddvar Eriksen and Lars Inge Terum on a research project funded by the Research Council of Norway (NFR). These ideas have been further developed and to some extent applied in another NFR-funded research project titled "Social Security in Context: Fairness, Efficiency, and Distribution."

Before Harald died, we had been working on a manuscript summarizing our research and teaching on discretion, and it was my task to produce a new version of it during the spring of 2011. However, this work was put on hold, as I was unsure about how to proceed without Harald. During a stay at the European University Institute in Florence in the spring of 2012, I resumed the project, and since then, I have worked on it whenever my schedule has permitted it, albeit with a certain sense of uneasiness about proceeding on my own with what was a cooperative project. Without a doubt, this would have been a different (and longer) book if Harald had not passed away, but what is presented is approaches and arguments we developed together, and I think he would have agreed to most of what is said – or rather I think he would not have disagreed. I cannot remember Harald saying "I agree"; he always said, "I don't disagree." I initially added Harald as a coauthor, but was advised by colleagues not to do so since I have to answer for this book. However, I have retained the use of "we."

The book uses material from earlier publications. Chapters 1 and 2 include material from our article "Understanding Discretion" in *Sociology of Professions: Continental and Anglo-Saxon Traditions*, edited by Lennart G. Svensson and Julia Evetts (Gothenburg: Daidalos, 2010), and from a longer Norwegian version ("Profesjon og skjønn" [Professions and Discretion]) in *Profesjonsstudier*, edited by Anders Molander and Lars Inge Terum (Oslo: Universitetsforlaget, 2008). The section on discretionary space in

Chapter 2 is based on a paper that we presented in a seminar at the Centre for the Study of Professions in Oslo in December 2010. Chapters 3 and 4 include material from Anders Molander, Harald Grimen, and Erik Oddvar Eriksen, "Professional Discretion and Accountability in the Welfare State" in *Journal of Applied Philosophy* (29, no. 3), and from Anders Molander, "Profesjonelt skjønn i velferdsstaten: mekanismer for ansvarliggjøring" [Professional discretion in the welfare state: mechanisms of accountability] in *Profesjonsstudier II*, edited by Anders Molander and Jens Christian Smeby (Oslo: Universitetsforlaget, 2013).

I have had the privilege of working with Lisa Wallander on the subject of discretion. Our cooperation has resulted in two articles: Lisa Wallander and Anders Molander, "Disentangling Professional Discretion: A Conceptual and Methodological Approach" in *Professions and Professionalism* (2014, no. 3), and "Learning to Reason: The Factorial Survey as a Teaching Tool in Social Work Education" in *Nordic Social Work Research* (forthcoming). Lisa not only introduced me to the factorial survey approach, a method for analyzing judgments on which she is an expert, but also contributed to the conceptual analysis presented in this book.

I am thankful to Cathrine Holst for her feedback on earlier drafts, to Erik Oddvar Eriksen for initiating the aforementioned research project and to Lars Inge Terum for pushing me not to abandon it all to the "gnawing criticism of the mice," as Marx once said.

# Introduction

Professionalization is one of the distinctive features of modern societies. More and more occupational groups with some of the characteristics of the classical professions (medicine and law) have arisen, and the number of professionals has grown dramatically. An important part of this growth has occurred within the domains of the welfare state and resulted in a diverse group of so-called welfare state professions.[1]

There are different ways of defining professions, but the essential characteristic of professional occupations is that they provide expert services. The knowledge and skills applied are acquired through a formal higher education based on different scientific disciplines as well as established know-how. Hence, there is an asymmetry between professionals and the recipients of their services who lack this expertise but are in need of these services for solving certain practical problems in their lives. This asymmetry makes trust important in professions' relationships with the public. As Adam Smith remarked, "We trust our health to the physician; our fortune and sometimes our life and reputation to the lawyer and attorney."[2] The exclusivity over tasks related to various vital human goods that professions are granted through political and legal regulations gives rise to corresponding fiduciary responsibilities on their side.[3] This arrangement has been termed "the grand bargain" between the professions and the public.[4] However, there is also another picture of the professions, namely, that they are primarily occupational groups that aim to monopolize the provision of particular services so as to gain economic advantages.[5] As Smith also commented, "People of the same trade seldom meet together, even for merriment and diversion, but the conversation ends in a conspiracy against the public, or in some contrivance to raise prices."[6] An adequate theory of professions must capture both sides of the professions, the fiduciary role as well as the self-serving search for occupational control. Professions essentially constitute an ambiguous phenomenon, located between two worlds, so to speak: between trust and morality on the one hand and between money and group-interests on the other.

2   *Introduction*

In this book, we are concerned with the use of discretion that is associated with the fiduciary role of professions. When professions are entrusted with the task of applying knowledge to particular cases, they are also entrusted with discretionary power. More specifically, we are concerned with one type of professional discretion, namely, discretion exercised by professionals who act as "street-level bureaucrats" in the welfare state.[7] As street-level bureaucrats, members of different professions (e.g., physicians, nurses, psychologists, social workers, teachers) directly (or indirectly) provide public benefits and services in face-to-face relationships with citizens, for example, income support, health and social services, and education. Welfare state professionals decide or establish premises as to whom will receive what, in what manner, when and how much, and when enough is enough. They control who passes through the gates of the welfare state. They are authorized to solve problems on behalf of the state, with specified means, for certain purposes, in certain areas, based on special knowledge and methodologies sanctioned by a prescribed certification system. They allocate huge resources, and their judgments and decisions affect people's lives, often in very sensitive areas. Laws regulate their activities; however, legal rules are often indeterminate, granting street-level bureaucrats quite extensive discretionary powers. The tasks they carry out are such that political authorities cannot specify exactly what the problems are, exactly what to do, and exactly how much resources to deploy in particular cases. The power, as well as the responsibility entailed, to make such judgments and decisions is delegated to professionals. Accordingly, the role of professions in the welfare state can be analyzed in terms of so-called principal–agent relationships,[8] where the agent acts on behalf of another, the principal (in this case, the public), and is supposed to serve the principal's interests. The public appears as the principal in a double sense here: on the one hand, it gives the professions their mandate; on the other hand, it (or individual members of the public) seeks the help of the professionals they have mandated.

The delegation of discretionary power to welfare state professionals to make judgments and decisions regarding who is entitled to what is one aspect of a more general trend of growing discretionary powers. This trend has been characterized as "perhaps the most significant twentieth century change in the fundamentals of the legal system,"[9] moving it away from the rule of law ideal of a regular and predictable exercise of public authority.[10] To what extent the allocation of benefits and services should depend on professional judgment is therefore a key issue in the normative theory of the welfare state.[11] The argument for discretion is based on the necessity of ensuring flexibility and adaptability to individual needs and circumstances. By contrast, the argument for reducing the latitude for discretion is that discretion can be abused and can lead to arbitrariness and domination. However, eliminating discretion is simply not possible. It would require the specification of general rules for all benefits and services distributed by the welfare state in such a way that entitlement in particular cases could be a matter of subsumption. Although it is possible to make certain benefits unconditional, many of them will remain more or less subject to an assessment of needs and circumstances. With regard to welfare services, the element of discretion cannot be eliminated – it can be made only more or less extensive.

In the literature on professions, discretion is described as a core characteristic of professional work.[12] Discretion is seen as an unavoidable aspect of the practice of applying general knowledge, embedded in "if–then" rules, to particular cases.[13] All professions apply such knowledge in one form or another, and what is more, they are authorized to do so. However, when general rules do not determine unambiguous conclusions about what ought to be done in particular cases, one must use judgment, the argument goes. This feature of professional work has been seen as an important basis for what Andrew Abbott calls the "jurisdictional claims" of professions, that is, claims for "the legitimate control of a particular kind of work."[14] Without some degree of indeterminacy, tasks could be carried out mechanically, and it would not matter who carried them out. However, if the knowledge that qualifies individuals to carry out such tasks could not be systematized, standardized, learned, and communicated, there would be no basis for a formal education program that offers certification, which is a characteristic feature of professions. The claim for professional status then presupposes a kind of knowledge that can be standardized and transmitted as well as a degree of indeterminacy when this knowledge is applied.

Despite the important role played by discretion in models of professionalism, the sociology literature on professions has astonishing little to say about discretion. It is often just a residual notion that is contrasted negatively with clear-cut decision rules. Moreover, discretion is rarely discussed as a normative problem. Although necessary because of the "indeterminacy intrinsic in highly specialized tasks,"[15] professional discretion also involves different sorts of risks.[16] When professions are entrusted with discretionary power, the premise is that they will use this power in a responsible way, and ethical codes express commitments on their part to reduce such agency risks.[17] The efficacy of ethical codes as devices of professional self-regulation may be questioned, but they are nevertheless "promises" that professions give in exchange for their publicly granted jurisdictions.[18] However, within the ethics of professions, relatively little attention has been paid to discretion and accountability compared with the literature on public administration, particularly welfare administration, where the implications of street-level discretion regarding the treatment of citizens and democratic governance is an important concern.[19]

In this book, we provide an analysis of discretion and apply it to the challenges created by the extensive use of professional discretion in the implementation of welfare law and policies. Our guiding thread is a distinction between *discretionary space* and *discretionary reasoning* – or, as we also say, between discretion in a *structural* sense and discretion in an *epistemic* sense. On the one hand, discretion can be understood as a space for making decisions based on one's own judgment. Discretion, in this sense, is an "opportunity-concept." The area of discretion consists of those courses of action that are permissible. When agents are entrusted to make autonomous judgments and decisions, one talks about discretionary power. They are authorized to act on behalf of somebody, or in someone's interest, to whom they are also accountable. On the other hand, discretion can be understood as an "exercise-concept" that refers to the cognitive activity performed within such spaces, that is, reasoning under conditions of indeterminacy.[20]

The distinction between discretion and epistemic discretion is essential from a normative point of view. When discretionary power is delegated, the presumption is that the entrusted actor is capable of performing the involved tasks and will do so judiciously. This means that the actor's judgments, decisions, and actions are expected to result from a process of reasoning and, therefore, to be supported by good reasons. Moreover, these reasons must qualify as public reasons. Professionals are granted discretionary power because of their certified knowledge, and they are expected to justify their decisions by referring to this knowledge as well as to laws and generally accepted principles. Therefore, discretion is also accompanied by a demand for accountability – that is, individuals can be held to account for their judgments and decisions. In the end, this is what distinguishes discretionary authority from arbitrary power.

There are certainly numerous instances where discretion is exercised sloppily, with many of these instances probably remaining undetected and unsanctioned. However, the problem with discretion extends much deeper; it is not limited to negligent conduct. Even conscientious professionals are fallible, and their reasoning may contain distortions caused by, for example, the use of heuristics. Like all humans, they may turn out to be what we shall later call "nonideal reasoners." However, even "ideal reasoners," who, by definition, do not make cognitive errors, may draw different conclusions regarding the same case. This possibility is inherent in discretion as a form of reasoning. Reasonable disagreement might be expected to occur because the form of reasoning contains some noneliminable sources of variation. This is what we call the "burdens of discretion."

In the first chapter, we take a look at how discretion has been justified and the challenges that have been identified by its critics so as to create a backdrop for our own analysis of the two dimensions of discretion in the second chapter. In the third chapter, we turn our attention to the discretion exercised by members of different professions when they act as gatekeepers of the welfare state. In this role, they make judgments and decisions (or establish premises for decisions) regarding access to benefits and services. For many welfare rights, the eligibility criteria are vague, and discretion is necessary to determine who has a right to $X$. This may also apply to the entitlement clauses that specify what one is entitled to, when one has a right or a legitimate claim to $X$. Rights that are in some way discretionary give professionals a more or less extensive discretionary power. The legislator leaves it up to them to assess who is entitled to what.

The delegation of discretionary powers to professionals as street-level bureaucrats in the welfare state is troublesome because doing so is in tension with the demands of the rule of law and democratic authority. When professionals are entrusted to judge, decide, and act more or less autonomously, this situation may threaten a core principle of the rule of law, namely, the formal principle of justice or equal treatment. Similar cases should be treated similarly, and different cases should be treated differently. If cases are treated differently, relevant differences must be present. Even if professionals carry out their assessments properly, they may judge the same case differently. The tension associated with democratic rule arises from the fact that it is difficult for political bodies to survey, control, and govern the use of this discretionary power and that professionals' own best judgment may be based on premises that are not authorized by those bodies. The worry is that what occurs in a discretionary space lacks democratic legitimacy.

A welfare state that distributes benefits and services based on need is dependent on the use of discretionary judgments. The two tensions are then of an intrinsic character. They cannot be eliminated without first giving up the welfare state as it is currently known. However, these tensions can be ameliorated, and in the fourth chapter, we discuss mechanisms of accountability, that is, measures for ensuring a judicious and responsible use of discretionary powers. It is common to distinguish between such mechanisms based on their direction: mechanisms that work vertically (top to bottom, and vice versa) or horizontally (e.g., collegiality), and ones that work from the outside (external control) or from within (self-regulation). Based on our distinction between discretion in the structural and epistemic senses, we test another approach. In line with this distinction, we differentiate between two main types of accountability mechanisms – structural and epistemic – that cut across the standard classifications and set the focus on the connection between accountability and the demand for justification. Structural mechanisms restrict the scope for discretion or put restrictions on the behavior of actors with discretionary authority, whereas epistemic mechanisms focus on improving the conditions for and the quality of discretionary reasoning. We outline five subtypes of each of the two types of mechanisms. Although the two lists are not exhaustive, and the boundaries between structural and epistemic mechanisms (as well as between the different subtypes) are not entirely clear, they still illustrate an approach to the issues of professional discretion and accountability that we believe is worth pursuing.

## Notes

1 Ramsøy and Kjølsrød (1986).
2 Smith (1776/1976, 122). In modern economics, the importance of trust relations in medical services has been emphasized by Arrow (1963).
3 That fiduciary responsibilities follow from the informational or epistemic asymmetry between professionals (as experts) and the recipients of their services (as laypeople) was underlined by Parsons (1978). See also Sciulli (2009, chap. 9) and Heath (2014, chap. 3).
4 Sedulsky and Sedulsky (2015, 21–23).
5 This is the focus of an influential tradition in the sociology of professions, cf. Larson (1977) and Macdonald (1995), as well as of market liberal accounts of professions, cf. Friedman (1962).
6 Smith (1776/1976, 145).
7 Lipsky (1980), Adler and Asquith (1981), Brodkin (1997), Vinzant and Crothers (1998), Brodkin (2013), and Hupe et al. (2015). Regarding administrative justice at the front line, see also Mashaw (1983).
8 Buchanan (1988) and Buchanan (1996).
9 Davis (1969, 20).
10 Scheuerman (1994).
11 Goodin (1988, chap. 7).
12 See, for example, Freidson (2001) and Miller (2010, chap. 6). According to Jamous and Peloille (1970, 112), professions are occupational groups whose "indetermination/technicality ratio" is "generally high" ("technicality" represents "means that can be mastered in the form of rules").
13 See Mashaw (1983, 26–29, 31–32).
14 Abbott (1988, 60).
15 Sharma (1997, 771).
16 Shapiro (1987), Sharma (1997) and Shapiro (2005).
17 Arrow (1963) and Buchanan (1988).
18 Eriksen (2015).
19 For an overview of this literature, see Meyers and Vorsanger (2003) and Hill (2005, chap. 12).
20 The terms *opportunity-concept* and *exercise-concept* are borrowed from Charles Taylor (1986).

# 1 Discretion and its critics

The origin of the English word *discretion* is the Latin word *discretus*, a form of the verb *discernere*, which means to separate, discern, or distinguish. In *Leviathan* (1651), Thomas Hobbes made an inventory of different intellectual virtues, with discretion being one of them. Discretion, he stated, involves "Distinguishing and Discerning, and Judging between Thing and Thing," especially in cases where "such Discerning is not easie."[1] To distinguish between "Thing and Thing" is to judge according to some standard: one claims that some object has or does not have a certain property or set of properties. In this sense, one can make judgments, for instance, about objects like utterances, actions, states, or products. A judgment can involve a claim that an utterance is "true" or "authentic," that an action is "efficacious" or "right," that a state is "normal," "desirable," or "just," or that a product is "good" (like a good knife) or "beautiful." Judgments distinguish true from false and authentic from inauthentic utterances; right from wrong and efficacious from nonefficacious actions; normal from abnormal, desirable from undesirable, and just from unjust states; and good from bad and beautiful from ugly products. However, as Hobbes noted, making such distinctions is not always easy. Here is a short list of reasons (ours, not those of Hobbes) of why it may be difficult:

1  *Identity of the "objects" (or "things")*. It is often not clear what the "object" of assessment is. The object can both be very complex and have fuzzy boundaries. For instance, when assessing an action's efficaciousness, one has to assess its consequences in relation to the intended aim or the agent's goal. However, an action's consequences can conflict and may have to be balanced against each other. All actions also have unintended and/or unrecognized side effects. Moreover, some effects are short term, and others are long term; some are proximal, and others are distal. Therefore, one must sort out the

relevant consequences. However, sorting out these consequences is not always easy and may arouse controversy. All this may make it difficult to judge whether an action has been efficacious for the simple reason that it is not clear where the boundaries of the object are. In a situation like this, it is not obvious what one actually wants to assess, how the "object" should be focused, and how it should be distinguished from other objects.

2   *Identity of the properties.* There often exists a lack of clear identification criteria for the properties that one is to ascribe (or to abstain from ascribing) to objects. For example, medical diagnostics lack unambiguous descriptions of many diseases (however, there are also, of course, clear descriptions of many diseases). Different diagnostic manuals contain different lists of symptoms, which often match only partially and incompletely – or not at all. Hence, observed symptoms can be difficult to subsume under existing diagnostic labels for the simple reason that it is not evident what existing diagnostic labels include and exclude. This difficulty is rampant in psychiatry. It may also be a problem in criminal justice. The way in which some crimes are described does not always make it clear what can and what cannot be subsumed under the various labels.

3   *Identity of the standards.* Standards used in assessments must be interpreted so as to obtain a hold on reality. For instance, what does it mean that something is normal? Is it something that is healthy in contrast to something that is pathological? Is it a statistical mean value, for example, the mean height or weight in a population? Does it mean something that no one notices because it is so entrenched in the trivialities of everyday life? Often several senses of normal can be relevant simultaneously. The same goes for standards such as justice and, of course, beauty. Standards must be interpreted so as to obtain a hold on reality, but interpretations often differ.

4   *Relevance.* It can be, and often is, unclear which standards are relevant in a particular case. Relevance itself is a very fuzzy concept, and the question of relevance is always connected to some goal or target of action. For instance, if one patient demands more nursing and care than other patients, which standard is relevant to assess this patient's claims? Should equal treatment with other patients be the right standard? If this is the relevant standard, one cannot give undue weight to one single patient's particular needs or claims. This patient's needs and claims must then always be balanced against the needs and claims of others. Or is the individualization of care and nursing the relevant standard here? Should this particular patient's needs and claims be satisfied without comparing them to the needs and claims of others? Is there a

sense in which one should be given one's due, without regard for the needs and claims of others at all? How should one select the relevant standard in such a situation?

These four issues illustrate why discretion is an "intellectual virtue," as Hobbes described it: discretion is required when "discerning is not easy." In addition to listing discretion as an intellectual virtue, Hobbes linked discretion to civil liberty, stating that "[i]n cases where the sovereign hath prescribed no rule, then the subject hath the liberty to do, or forbear, according to his own discretion."[2] In this sense, discretion involves possessing a *negative liberty*.[3] A negative liberty provides the actor with an area for choice and action consisting of those options that are neither forbidden nor prescribed.[4] The actor can freely choose between such alternatives without interference from others. An individual's negative liberty corresponds to the duty of others not to interfere with this individual's exercise of it. To have discretion in this sense is then to possess a restricted and protected space, where a certain kind of liberty to judge, decide, and act is granted.

This latter sense of discretion corresponds well with common contemporary definitions. In *Discretionary Powers*, legal scholar D. J. Galligan states, "To have discretion is, then, in its broadest sense, to have a sphere of autonomy within which one's decisions are in some degree a matter of personal judgment and assessment."[5] In a narrower sense, discretion does not designate the autonomy of legal subjects per se, but rather a power

> delegated within a system of authority to officials or a set of officials, where they have some significant scope for settling the reasons and standards according to which that power is to be exercised, and for applying them in the making of specific decisions.[6]

According to Aharon Barak, discretion is the power "given to a person with authority to choose between two or more alternatives, when each of the alternatives is lawful."[7] Jeffrey Jowell defines it as "the room for decisional manoeuvre possessed by a decision-maker."[8] In his influential book *Discretionary Justice*, Kenneth C. Davis states, "A public officer has discretion whenever the effective limits on this power leave him free to make a choice among possible courses of action or inaction."[9] In a discussion on discretion in the welfare state, Robert Goodin defines it as "an area of conduct which is generally governed by rules but where the dictates of the rules are indeterminate. In short, discretion refers, negatively, to a lacuna in a system of rules."[10] In the same vein, Keith Hawkins says that discretion "might be regarded as the space, as it were, between legal rules in which legal actors may exercise choice."[11] Several other definitions, all pointing in the same direction, could be quoted here. A common element of these definitions is the "embedded character of discretion."[12] This is well expressed in Ronald Dworkin's famous doughnut metaphor. Discretion, he says, is like "the hole in a doughnut, it does not exist except as an area left open by a surrounding belt of restriction."[13] To have discretion is to have an authority to decide in cases where rules and standards do not prescribe determinate results.

With Hobbes as our point of departure, we have identified two main ways of understanding discretion. In Robert Alexy's terms, we have distinguished between discretion in an epistemic sense and a structural sense.[14] *Epistemically*, discretion is a form of reasoning that results in judgments about the properties of various kinds of objects under conditions of indeterminacy or, according to Hobbes, where discerning is not easy. Indeterminacy means that the available reasons do not warrant one and only one outcome; hence, one must make use of one's own judgment to draw conclusions rather than relying on an algorithm.[15] This does not mean that any conclusion is possible. For example, the notion of a "hard case" in law denotes a case where the judge has to choose from among legally *acceptable* conclusions. Thus, indeterminacy has to be considered a gradual phenomenon, where full determinacy (i.e., there is only one possible outcome) and full indeterminacy (i.e., all possible outcomes are equally acceptable) mark the hypothetical end points of a continuum. When the subset of acceptable outcomes is not identical with all possible outcomes, one may describe this as a case of underdeterminacy.[16] *Structurally*, discretion is a space for decision-making and action-taking on the basis of discretionary judgments. To have discretion means to have a certain liberty or autonomy. To obtain a proper grasp of discretion and its challenges, one needs both the epistemic notion of *discretionary reasoning* and the structural notion of a *discretionary space*. We shall return to the analysis of discretion in the next chapter, but will first have a look at the standard arguments in favor of discretion as well as the concerns it has raised.[17]

## Justifying discretion

At least four different arguments for discretion can be distinguished. Some of these arguments are related to one another, but they are, nevertheless, distinct. In many accounts of discretion, several of these arguments are mixed, in one form or another. However, giving each of them a separate treatment can provide greater clarification. We do not intend to provide a historical account of how discretion has been justified. Our survey of the four ways of justifying discretion serves analytical, not historical, purposes.[18]

One way of justifying discretion dates back to Aristotle's discussion of legal justice in *The Nicomachean Ethics*. Aristotle's argument is based on a logical point about the relations between general statements and particular cases. According to Aristotle, "all law is universal, and there are some things about which it is not possible to pronounce rightly in general terms." When a law errs owing to its generality (i.e., it does not cover a case), Aristotle states that

> it is right . . . to correct the omission by a ruling such as the legislator himself would have given if he had been present there, and as he would have enacted if he had been aware of the circumstances.[19]

Aristotle uses the term *equity* when describing this rectification of legal justice. It fills the gap between the letter of the law and a particular case and allows for a fair adjudication. Sticking to the letter of the law, no matter what, can lead to grave injustice, as Cicero later pointed out in *On Duties*, referring to the saying *summum ius summa iniuria* (the more justice, the more injustice).[20] Samuel Pufendorf, the great seventeenth-century natural law scholar, followed in the footsteps of Aristotle, defining equity as

> a correction of the law where law is deficient through its universality; or a skilful interpretation of the law by which it is shown from natural reason that some particular case is not covered by a general law since an absurd situation would result if it were.[21]

This argument for discretion does not imply that discretion is unavoidable. However, it does imply that eliminating discretion leads to injustice, the kind of injustice that is created by those who stick to the letter of the law, no matter what. The cost of eliminating discretion is imperfect justice – or, perhaps in some cases, outright injustice. Based on this argument, *discretion corrects imperfections in a rule-oriented way of reasoning*.

A second way of justifying or accounting for discretion is built on the idea that discretion is necessary when rules do not give clear answers to practical questions. According to legal theorist H. L. A. Hart, it is a human predicament that whenever one tries to regulate some area of conduct, one cannot anticipate "all possible combinations of circumstances that the future may bring," and therefore, one cannot make general rules (e.g., legal rules), "the application of which to particular cases never called for a further choice."[22] Almost all rules "will, at some point where their application is in question, prove indeterminate; they will have . . . an *open texture*."[23] This argument takes its inspiration from Ludwig Wittgenstein's considerations on rule following.[24] However, it is important to keep in mind that the insight that rules do not determine their own application is not something exclusively Wittgensteinian. In fact, Immanuel Kant, the thinker of universal norms par préférence, also makes this point.[25] With regard to moral principles, he remarks that they "require a power of judgment sharpened by experience . . . in order to decide in which cases they apply."[26] This power of judgment, Kant writes in *The Critique of Pure Reason*, cannot be replaced by rules stating how to distinguish "whether something stands under a given rule or not" because "[t]his in turn, for the very reason it is a rule, again demands guidance from judgment."[27] What this means is that judgment or discretion belongs to the logic of rule application. It is something that is not possible to circumvent. Based on this argument, *discretion is a necessary part of all rule-following behavior.*

A third way of justifying discretion is based on the view that discretion is a mechanism for making decisions in situations characterized by a certain kind of complexity, meaning that there are no clear decision rules to follow. Let's say one has to choose between different options but is unsure about the consequences of the different options. Perhaps one is also in doubt about how to assess these consequences; in light of which criteria. In such a situation, one can rely on guidelines, but being able to make a good decision – or any decision – requires the use of one's judgment. This is a common way to justify and talk about discretion, both in decision theory and ordinary life. What makes discretion necessary is our "bounded rationality."[28] However, connecting discretion to complexity and claiming that complexity demands discretion can be problematic because relying on discretion, as we will see, may not be the best way to navigate complex decision situations. Anyway, based on this argument, discretion is necessary *for making good decisions – or any decisions at all – when there are no clear decision rules.*

A fourth way of justifying discretion is based on the claim that in so-called human processing and human changing activities, such as health care, teaching, and social work, adequate treatment requires individualization. One has to determine, all things considered, what is the best way of meeting the needs of patients, pupils, and clients. For example, Richard M. Titmuss argued that a welfare system requires discretion so as to adapt its benefits and services to the myriad of individual circumstances.[29] The argument is not that discretion corrects for or complements other kinds of reasoning but rather that it serves a good end (a proper treatment), allowing flexibility and sensitivity in dealing with the particular case. This argument says that if discretion is replaced by something else (e.g., universal rules, formulas), this goes against the logic of the activities in question. Based on this account, *discretion serves a certain purpose.*

## Worries about discretion

Discretion has its share of critics, however. There are at least two different kinds of criticism against discretion. One points to its possibly dismal effects and the difficulties of holding persons with discretion accountable and under control. A.V. Dicey, who is credited with having coined the term rule of law, views discretion as its opposite because "wherever there is discretion there is room for arbitrariness."[30] According to Friedrich A. Hayek, the problem of discretion is basically a problem of individual liberty. It is when "the administration interferes with the private sphere of the citizen" that discretion threatens to undermine the rule of law.[31] His view of the emerging welfare state was that this was exactly what was happening, and therefore, it was no less than a step on "the road to serfdom."[32] However, discretion is not solely a libertarian issue.[33] Promoters of the welfare state have viewed social rights as a means to eliminating or reducing the discretionary character of welfare benefits and services. Robert Goodin has systematized much of the worries about delegating discretionary power to welfare state professionals in gatekeeper positions.[34]

Another kind of criticism has been brought forward by cognition research. Here discretionary reasoning is considered to be less accurate than even simple formulas in probabilistic surroundings. Experimental studies seem to demonstrate that under certain circumstances, discretionary reasoning is outperformed by the application of formulas.[35] In complex decision situations, it can be simply very unwise to rely on discretionary judgments. As a backdrop for our own discussion, we shall explore these two kinds of criticisms a bit further.

With regard to the first kind of criticism, Goodin identifies four negative consequences of discretion in the context of the welfare state. Before we address these consequences, it is, however, important to note that Goodin's argument is premised upon what he calls "complete discretion."[36] To have complete discretion is to judge, decide, and act under no constraints whatsoever de jure and under no obligation to have any reasons whatsoever for how one acts. Complete discretion is formal (delegated), strong (no rules), and ultimate (no possible review or appeal). Persons with complete discretion must be forced to justify their decisions and actions. Only the threat of sanctions can force them to behave in a decent way; otherwise, they will do so only if they want to.

It must also be noted that Goodin does not provide any good examples of discretion working well. The reason may be because there are no such examples, but the imbalance in Goodin's analysis leads one to suspect that he has picked his examples so as to create a worst-case scenario. There is nothing wrong per se with worst-case scenarios – they can be very illuminating. However, as with all such scenarios, one may ask how realistic or representative they are. Owing to the pervasiveness of discretion in welfare states, it is simply very difficult to judge the representativeness of Goodin's examples. Many have had negative experiences with professionals or officials with discretionary powers, but to be sure, not all experiences with professionals or officials with discretionary powers are negative.

One negative consequence of discretion is that it can lead to *manipulation* and *exploitation*. Goodin explains,

> [I]t is in one sense the classic objection to one person's having discretionary control over the disposition of resources which another person needs that that person thereby acquires *power* over the other. Such a person can lay down all sorts of demands and back them up with threats to withhold the needed resources from the other unless that person complies with those demands.[37]

Administrators of welfare programs, for instance, can use their discretionary powers to impose standards of morality on welfare recipients. They can do this simply because they control the resources that the recipients need, and if discretion is complete, there are no constraints that can stop them from imposing stricter standards or their own personal standards of morality on the recipients.

Another negative consequence of discretion is that it can lead to *arbitrariness*. Goodin states,

> Insofar as someone enjoys complete (strong, formal, ultimate) discretionary control over some matter, then it follows from the definitions offered . . . that that person is not obliged to have, much less to give, any reasons whatsoever for deciding one way or another.[38]

It follows from Goodin's definition of complete discretion that the decisions of persons with this kind of discretion must be arbitrary because they are not obliged to give reasons, only to demonstrate that it was within their right to do so. Whether there are or have been persons with complete discretion in Goodin's sense is another matter, however. Officials may have had complete de facto discretion, but only sovereigns may have had complete de jure discretion.

Yet another negative consequence of discretion is that it can lead to *uncertainty*, *unpredictability*, and *insecurity*. Goodin points out that

> [i]nsofar as some matter is completely discretionary, and depends wholly upon some official's own arbitrary will, those who are subject to the decision will have no good way of predicting what the outcome will be. At most, they might try to make some inferences based on the official's past practices.[39]

## Discretion and its critics 15

The mechanism behind such uncertainty, unpredictability, and insecurity is the simple fact that because persons with complete discretionary powers do not need to have any reasons for what they decide, there are no compelling reasons for them to behave in a particular way. They can follow their own arbitrary will, as Goodin says. Hence, one cannot expect similar decisions in the future, even from the same person. If individuals do not need to have any reasons for how they have acted in the past, there are no particular reasons to expect that they will act in some specific way in the future. Or, to express it differently, there are no good reasons to expect individuals to feel committed to or bound by their own past decisions. Persons who do not need to have any reasons whatsoever for what they do become unpredictable to others (and maybe to themselves). Others cannot infer how they will act in the future from the reasons that they have given for their actions in the past.

Finally, discretion can lead to illegitimate *intrusion into people's privacy*. Goodin notes,

> The ethos of discretionary judgments is that they are able to be made on the basis of the "full facts" of the particular case: such decisions are to be made with reference to "the case in the round," rather than with reference to some selective aspects of it artificially isolated by some narrow rules, and so on. Now, if this advantage is to accrue, officials guided by discretion must necessarily base their decisions on more information about individual claimants than would officials guided by rules alone.[40]

Goodin raises two important points here. The first point can be illustrated by reference to one of the justifications of discretion mentioned previously – namely, that discretion serves the morally good end of individualized treatment. If the advantages of individualized interventions are to accrue, then officials must, implicitly at least, be permitted to collect all the information that is necessary so as to make interventions truly individualized. They must, so to speak, be permitted to find or locate the true individual. The second point is simply that individuals who have complete discretion have no such limits on what information they can gather. Their only stopping point is their own judgment about when they have collected enough information to close the case or about when they have obtained "the full facts" of the case. Goodin may, however, be chasing a chimera here. If modern cognition research is to be believed, then individuals exercising discretionary reasoning seldom decide on the basis of the full facts of a case. They rapidly select a few salient features of the situation and decide on the basis of this.

Another risk can be added to Goodin's list: *discrimination*. The exercise of discretion may result in differential treatment that is arbitrary in the

16  *Discretion and its critics*

sense that it is not justified by relevant differences. If persons who share some salient but irrelevant characteristic are systematically disadvantaged, discretion amounts to discrimination. Instead of formal rules determining outcomes, there are informal factors or mechanisms, operating illegitimately in the discretionary space, that make outcomes less unpredictable. Hence, discretionary outcomes may have a sociological pattern even if they are not formally predictable. M. P. Baumgartner concludes that "the more discretion there is, the more completely case outcomes will be determined by social factors that vary from case to case, and the more systematically advantaged some people will be to others."[41]

According to Goodin, the only way to avoid the dismal consequences of discretion is to abolish it. Goodin poses the following question: "Is there any way to overcome the problems with discretion . . . that does not entail depriving officials of discretion?" He then immediately answers his own question, stating, "I shall argue that the answer is no. The problems are inherent in the practice of discretion and can be overcome (if at all) only by removing discretion from officials."[42] However, he also claims that discretion cannot be abolished, that it cannot be removed from officials in welfare states. Here discretion is necessarily pervasive, owing to the nature of the benefits and services that such states allocate. Welfare states that aim to protect people against social risks are also, if Goodin is correct, at risk of engaging in misrule.

Another legal-political concern about the exercise of street-level discretion that is not discussed by Goodin involves democratic governance. In principal–agent terms, the delegation of discretionary power imposes different types of agency risks on democratic authorities (i.e., risks that law and policies may not be implemented as intended). Bo Rothstein describes the democratic problem as follows:

> [I]t is impossible . . . for central political organs to prescribe in detail all of the disparate measures which must be taken in each of the various cases to be handled. Accordingly, the operative staff who work face-to-face with clients – teachers, health staff, social workers, police, etc. – must be granted a relatively wide freedom of action, for it is they who must choose exactly which measures to apply in the individual case. . . . It is the sum of their actions which constitutes the public program. As to whether these actions reflect the objectives laid down by the democratically constituted organs – this must be regarded as an open question.[43]

If a democratic lawgiver "must" delegate discretionary powers so as to provide "case-by-case" management, an unavoidable tension appears not only with the principle of equal treatment, but also with democratic governance itself: representatives of the people give up control over how laws and policies are implemented, thereby affecting the lives of citizens.

The second main kind of criticism of discretion is very different and stems mainly from modern cognition research and the psychology of judgment and decision-making. According to this research, humans tend to determine what the case is or what something is or how probable future events are on the basis of heuristics (i.e., mental shortcuts) that are normally very useful but can lead to systematic and severe errors in some cases.[44] Heuristics are fallacious inference rules (they are mainly fallacious in the sense that they overgeneralize) but nevertheless hit the target (i.e., result in correct conclusions) most of the time and are at work subconsciously most of the time. Humans have a limited capacity for information processing and to a large extent use heuristics to bridge the gap between information and conclusions. Discretionary reasoning is influenced by such heuristics. Normally they work well, but because they are fallacious rules of inference, they can lead one seriously astray and cause fatal errors under certain circumstances (e.g., diagnostic errors).[45] Moreover, as we will see in the next chapter, discretionary reasoning is influenced by factors that are also at work under ideal conditions and do not imply cognitive errors.

The insight that human thinking and decision-making to a large extent depend on heuristics is not new. It was already couched in Herbert Simon's concept of bounded rationality.[46] However, present-day knowledge about heuristics is much richer, much more detailed, and much more precise than it was when Simon wrote his seminal works. It seems to be well documented that not only laypeople, but also experts have a tendency to commit such errors and, moreover, to be overconfident. We shall suggest that the best way of approaching heuristics in discussions about discretion is to treat them as a special kind of warrant, fulfilling the role as a bridge between premises and conclusions in discretionary reasoning. We shall return to this issue in Chapter 2. We shall also suggest in Chapter 4 that the influence of heuristics in discretionary reasoning must be taken into account in discussions of accountability.

## Notes

1. Hobbes (1979, 33).
2. Hobbes (1979, 115).
3. Berlin (1969).
4. Alexy (1994, 198 ff).
5. Galligan (1986, 8).
6. Galligan (1986, 21).
7. Barak (1989, 7).
8. Jowell (1973, 179).
9. Davis (1969, 4).
10. Goodin (1988, 186).
11. Hawkins (1992).
12. Hill (2005, 206).
13. Dworkin (1977, 31).
14. Alexy (2002, 393).
15. Coleman and Leiter (1993).
16. Solum (2010).
17. See also Feldman (1992) and Schneider (1992).
18. One way of justifying discretion that we do not take into consideration, is the one associated with kadi justice (see Weber (1978, 976–978) and Schneider (1992). In kadi justice, decisions are made on a case-by-case basis, which is inconsistent with the demands of modern formal law. According to Max Weber, disputed individual cases are settled by "informal judgements rendered in terms of concrete ethical or other practical valuations. . . . *Kadi*-justice knows no rational 'rules of decision' (*Urteilsgründe*) whatever." Weber then notes that "pure *Kadi*-justice is represented in every prophetic dictum that follows the pattern: 'It is written . . ., but I say unto you'" (Weber 1978, 976, 978). An example of kadi justice is the Solomonic judgment that was issued to settle a dispute between two women who had each laid claim to a baby as her own: "When all Israel heard the verdict the king had given, they held the king in awe, because they saw that he had wisdom from God to administer justice" (1 Kings 3:28).
19. Aristotle (1976, V, x, 199).
20. Cicero (1991, I, 10, 33).
21. Pufendorf (1673/1991, II, 10).
22. Hart (1961, 125).
23. Hart (1961, 124).
24. See Wittgenstein (1953, 185–241).
25. See O'Neill (1996, chap. 3, sec. 4) and Höffe (2001).
26. Kant (1785/1997, 5).
27. Kant (1781/1965, A132–3/171–2, 171). See also the introduction to "On the Common Saying: 'This May Be True in Theory, but It Does Not Apply in Practice'" (Kant 1991).
28. Simon (1957).
29. Titmuss (1971). See also Handler (1986) and Rothstein (1998, chap. 4).
30. Dicey (1885, 110).
31. Hayek (1960, 187).
32. Hayek (1944, chap. 6).
33. Scheuerman (1994).
34. Goodin (1988, chap. 7).

35 Kirkebøen (2009). The classical study is Meehl (1954).
36 Goodin (1988, 193).
37 Goodin (1988, 193).
38 Goodin (1988, 198).
39 Goodin (1988, 201).
40 Goodin (1988, 203).
41 See Baumgartner (1992).
42 Baumgartner (1992, 204).
43 Rothstein (1998, 80).
44 Connolly et al. (1999) and Gilovich et al. (2002). For overviews of this research tradition, see the introduction to Gilovich et al. (2002) and Keren and Teigen (2009). A masterful popularization is Kahneman (2011).
45 This is the main focus of the discussions among physicians about cognitive biases and diagnostic errors. See, for instance, Croskerry (2005) and Groopman (2007).
46 Simon (1957).

# 2 The anatomy of discretion

As we have seen, the use of spatial terms is pervasive in definitions of discretion. To have discretion means to have a space for judgment and decision-making. "Space for" refers to what an agent is allowed to do, given a set of rules and standards, while "judgment and decision-making" refers to the cognitive activity carried out by an agent within this space. Making judgments and decisions involves reasoning, and we expect agents with discretionary power to act on the basis of their *best* judgment, which means that their actions are supported by *good* reasons. Accordingly, we have made a distinction between *discretionary space* and *discretionary reasoning* – or, in Robert Alexy's terms, between discretion in a structural sense and discretion in an epistemic sense.[1] Here we shall sketch a conceptual framework that captures both aspects of discretion and elucidates Ronald why professional discretion may be normatively problematic.

## Discretion as space

The spatial terms used in the structural definitions of discretion raise two important questions: how are areas of judgment and decision-making constituted? How should the freedom of judgment and action at stake be understood?

Let us take Dworkin's doughnut metaphor as our point of departure. Dworkin argues against a broad interpretation of discretion comprising any instance of the use of judgment in the application of rules or standards. According to Dworkin, "[t]he concept of discretion is at home in only one sort of context: when someone is in general charged with making decisions subject to standards set by a particular authority."[2] When "an area [is] left open by a surrounding belt of restriction," the agent has discretion.[3] This means that discretion is relative in two senses: it is relative to certain restrictions and to the authority that has imposed these restrictions.

To illustrate what it means that discretionary spaces are surrounded by different belts of restrictions and, thus, are more or less wide or open,

Dworkin uses the following two examples. In the first example, a sergeant is ordered to select the five most experienced soldiers for a task. In the second example, he is ordered to select five soldiers. The first order refers to a standard: the sergeant must choose the five *most experienced* soldiers. It can be difficult to know what that means and how the standard should be interpreted. (Should length of service or combat experience or both count?). However, the sergeant must do more than just select five soldiers. He must relate the amount of experience to a standard. This implies that some selection procedures are excluded. The sergeant cannot select five soldiers at random or use self-selection among the soldiers. These procedures will not – other than randomly – select the five most experienced soldiers. The second order contains no standard, other than the number of soldiers to be selected. Here the sergeant can proceed in many different ways, for instance, by conducting random selection or allowing self-selection among the soldiers. He can also, if he wishes, select the five most experienced soldiers, for instance, those who have the most combat experience. In the two examples, the sergeant operates within two discretionary spaces that are differently constituted. The first discretionary space is narrower than the second because the sergeant has fewer available selection procedures.

To have discretion, as Dworkin understands it, is then to have a freedom of choice *delegated* by an authority, which is relative to standards imposed by the same authority. It follows that individuals who have discretion are accountable for and can be asked to justify their decisions. They are *charged* by some authority with making certain kinds of decisions under certain kinds of constraints and are thus – in principle – accountable to this authority. However, the challenge is to explain in greater detail what this means. This challenge can best be met by contrasting two different hypothetical views of how discretionary spaces are constituted. We may refer to these two views as "two concepts of holes."[4] In a pure form, one could say that discretionary spaces can be constituted exclusively by either (I) negative liberties or (II) entrustment relations. The differences can (roughly) be outlined as follows:

I    Discretionary spaces as constituted *exclusively* by negative liberties

   If $A$ has a negative liberty with regard to $X$, then

   1   $A$ can do with $X$ what $A$ wants;
   2   $A$ is under no obligation to justify what $A$ does with $X$ to anyone;
   3   All others have a duty not to interfere with what $A$ does with $X$ (and $A$ has a corresponding duty to all others).

II Discretionary spaces as constituted *exclusively* by relations of entrustment

> If $B$ has entrusted $A$ with $X$, then
> 1  $A$ cannot do with $X$ what $A$ wants;
> 2  $A$ normally has an obligation to justify what $A$ does with $X$ to $B$;
> 3  $B$ has a right to interfere with what $A$ does with $X$.

These two accounts are in prima facie conflict with one another on all three points. It cannot both be true at the same time that $A$ can do what $A$ wants with $X$ and that $A$ cannot do what $A$ wants with $X$. Moreover, it cannot both be true at the same time that $A$ has an obligation to justify $A$'s actions to someone and that $A$ has no obligation to justify $A$'s actions to anyone. And it cannot both be true at the same time that all others have a duty not to interfere with what $A$ does with $X$ and that specific others have a right to interfere.

Some examples of discretionary spaces created by negative liberties are civil rights such as freedom of speech, religion, and movement. One is free, in the sense of not being hindered by prohibitions, and one is not obliged to justify how one uses this liberty.[5] Discretionary spaces granted to public officials and professionals in official roles, however, cannot be conceived as being constituted by negative liberties. The reason is that their freedom of judgment and decision-making is a delegated power. They are charged with the task of making certain decisions or of acting on delegated authority to settle certain issues and can be seen as agents for those to whom they are accountable. However, at the same time, those who are delegated authority have the right to decide and act on the basis of their *best judgment*.

If this is so, then, on the one hand, the concept of *entrustment* is needed to justify the demand for accountability. The exercise of pure negative liberties is by definition exempt from the demand for accountability. Negative liberties are constituted by rights to do what one wants, without having to justify one's actions to others or even to oneself. The demand for accountability is grounded in the fact that someone has been entrusted to decide for or act as an agent of a principal, who has a right to demand a justification for the judgments, decisions, and actions of the agent. Without entrustment, there is no demand for accountability.

On the other hand, what is delegated is the *opportunity* to decide and act on the basis of one's own best judgment. An agent's best judgment can possibly go against the intentions of those on whose behalf the agent is entrusted to judge, decide, and act. If this possibility is removed, there will be no space for autonomous judgment and then no discretionary space. The agent would resemble Montesquieu's image of judges in a constitutional order who function merely as the mouthpiece of the law.[6]

Thus, discretionary spaces consist of a mixture of opportunities to decide and act and of demands for justification. The opportunity is always restricted because those who have discretion are charged with making certain decisions and are *accountable to* or are obliged to *justify* their decisions to principals.[7]

The idea of negative liberties is intrinsically connected to an understanding of autonomy as a right to *noninterference*. Autonomy is here defined by reference to the existence of duties to refrain from interfering with judgments, decisions, and actions. A person who is autonomous in this sense is protected against interference from others. To have a negative liberty is to have a right to do what one wants without interference from the state, as long as one does not violate the rights of other persons. This can be given different interpretations: it can be a right to do what one desires without interference, to follow one's strongest moral convictions without interference, or to decide for oneself whether one wants to justify or account for one's decisions and actions to others. Strictly speaking then, to be autonomous is to be accountable to no one.[8] The fewer restrictions on one's opportunities for making judgments and decisions and taking action, the stronger is one's autonomy, and vice versa. The negative rights of citizens are constructed like this. One is free to do what is not forbidden by law, and the space left open is a space for discretion.

The discretionary space of officials and professionals, however, is constituted by acts of entrustment; thus, a demand for accountability exists. They are expected to follow their best judgment, not their strongest desires. One's best judgment can conflict with one's strongest desires. It is also important to note that no one's best judgment needs to be the *final* judgment.

The concept of autonomy that is in play when talking about the delegated discretion of officials and professionals does not primarily emphasize noninterference, but rather the *capacity or ability to make good judgments*. What a good judgment is and whether a judgment is good are often controversial issues. The crucial point is, however, that the decisions and actions of individuals who lack the capacity to make good judgments are heteronomous. Their decisions and actions are governed by the judgments of others, not their own. However, this does not mean that autonomous judgments are independent of the judgments of others. Because the best judgment of individuals can be inferior to the best judgment of others, one may need others to serve as critics so as to arrive at one's own best judgment. Moreover, the full exercise of the capacity of individuals to judge can be critically dependent on the quality of the arguments encountered in their environment. A lack of access to the good judgments of others may hamper individuals' capacity for judging.

The entrustment of judgments, decisions, and actions to others is based on expectations about the agent's autonomy in this sense – that is, the ability or capacity of the agent to make good judgments. It is often couched in expectations about adequate competence. Entrusting something to someone who has demonstrated a lack of capacity to make good judgments is not reasonable. Entrustment confers liberties of judgment and decision-making on the basis of expected abilities.

What we have said implies that discretionary spaces are inherently ambiguous and riddled with tension. First, to have discretion is to be granted a liberty. On the one hand, it is not a license to do what one wants. One is entrusted to make certain kinds of judgments and decisions and to carry out certain kinds of actions on behalf of a delegating authority that can hold one to account. On the other hand, a discretionary space is an area that is "left open" to those who possess discretionary powers to choose what to do based on their best judgment. This situation creates a tension between liberty and accountability.

Second, two kinds of autonomy are in play: on the one hand, the freedom to choose between courses of action based on one's best judgment; on the other hand, the capacity to judge. The freedom to choose can be granted to someone. However, the capacity to judge cannot be granted to someone; it must come from other sources, for instance, education. It is possible to have the freedom to judge, but to lack the capacity. It is also possible to have the capacity to judge, but to lack the freedom to judge. One's freedom to judge is relative to external constraints, for instance, laws, rules, or threats of sanctions. One's capacity to judge can be reduced, for example, by a lack of competence and by various kinds of internal constraints (e.g., fear).

Third, in most kinds of professional judgments, there is a complicated interplay between formally authorized discretionary judgments and informal, nonauthorized discretionary judgments. To reach adequate settlements in concrete cases, professionals go beyond what can be inferred from validated knowledge and from legal and administrative rules. It is probably not possible to constrain a discretionary space so that only authorized judgments come out of it or only authorized beliefs, norms, or values influence the reasoning process.

## Discretion as reasoning

The spatial or structural dimension of discretion is inextricably linked with discretion in an epistemic sense. The entrustment of discretionary power to professionals – that is, the provision of a *space* to professionals so that they can make decisions in accordance with their own judgment – is based on the assumptions that discretionary judgments and decisions are not mere whimsies but are justifiable and that the practitioners involved are capable of making reasoned judgments and decisions. The expectation placed on these professionals is that they act in accordance with their *best* judgment, which means that what they do is supported by *good* reasons. Hence, this epistemic dimension of discretion – discretion as reasoning – is fundamental from a normative point of view.

A fully adequate analysis of discretion as reasoning does not exist, as far as we know. To be considered fully adequate, this type of analysis has to do the following:

1  It must exhibit the characteristic features of discretion as a kind of reasoning. Discretionary reasoning is a form of practical reasoning that aims to reach conclusions about what ought to be done in particular cases;[9] however, the *warrants are weak*, as we shall say.
2  It must lay bare the kinds of conditions under which discretionary reasoning is unavoidable. We call such conditions the *circumstances of discretion*, which are sources of indeterminacy that necessitate discretionary reasoning.
3  It must identify the normative frames or principles by which discretionary reasoning is bounded. We call such frameworks the *normative contexts of discretion*. These are general normative constraints, which differentiate between different kinds of discretionary reasoning.
4  It must explain why discretionary reasoning can be *normatively problematic*. Factors that create variation in the results of discretionary reasoning conducted under ideal conditions (i.e., when discretionary reasoning is carried out as thoroughly and conscientiously as possible) are referred to here as the *burdens of discretion*. When the fact that humans are nonideal reasoners who are exposed to cognitive bias is taken into account, the burdens of discretionary reasoning increase.

*Reasoning with weak warrants*

Professionals are concerned about two basic sets of questions in their work – questions about what is the case and questions about what ought to be done. Whereas answers to the former type of questions consist of diagnostic judgments that define the problems to be handled, answers to the latter type of questions prescribe actions (i.e., they say what the treatment should be, given a certain diagnosis). When professionals try to find accountable answers to these two types of questions, they are engaged in reasoning. To reason means to construct arguments or, alternatively expressed, to infer conclusions from a set of premises. The basic building blocks of reasoning can be illustrated by means of Stephen Toulmin's argument model.[10] According to Toulmin, an argument consists of three basic elements: (1) the *conclusion* or *claim* about something (C), (2) the *data* (D) that are used as a point of departure for making the claim, and (3) the *warrant* (W), which licenses the step from D to C. A warrant has the general form "if D, then C" – that is, given some data, one is entitled to draw the conclusion or make the claim C. The connections among the three elements can be illustrated as follows:

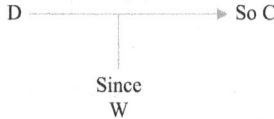

Toulmin illustrates this model with the following claim: "Harry is a British subject." This claim is supported by the datum "Harry was born in Bermuda" and the warrant "A man born in Bermuda will be a British subject." Furthermore, and as illustrated below, in the full model of the argument, the conclusion, datum, and warrant are accompanied by another three components. Both the *rebuttal* (R; "unless") and the *qualifier* (Q) deal with the specification of the conclusion. Whereas the conditions of rebuttal comprise various circumstances in which a particular warrant is not (or is less) applicable, the qualifier indicates the overall strength of the warrant. Finally, one or several *backings* (B; "on account of") may be denoted, the aim of which is to justify a certain warrant.

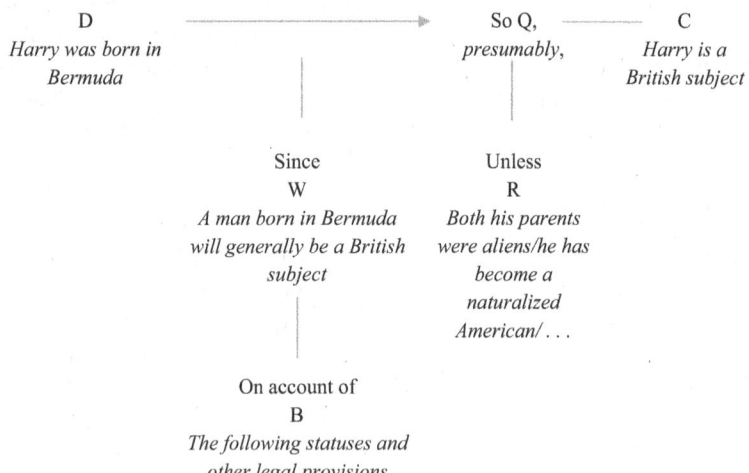

Let us apply this model to the two types of questions mentioned previously with which professions are confronted. In accordance with Toulmin's argument model, professionals need to combine a set of data (about a person or a situation) with one or several warranting if–then rules so as to come to a conclusion (make a claim) about the nature of the case at issue: if certain features occur, then there is a situation of type S. These inference rules can be referred to as *identification rules*. They bridge the gap between data and conclusions about what is the case (diagnosis). Subsequently, in coming to a conclusion (and making a claim) about what – if any – action to take so as to solve the problem(s) involved, the practitioners must combine this conclusion or diagnosis, which now comprises a second set of data, with one or several action norms specifying which intervention is the most appropriate given the circumstances. These norms may be called *treatment rules*. They are warrants bridging the gap between diagnosis and conclusions about what to do. When professionals – for example, general practitioners (GPs) and social workers – act as gatekeepers in the welfare state, they should also determine which individuals are eligible to receive certain benefits and to what they are entitled. In this case, treatment rules of a clinical and legal type are mixed.

Both identification rules and treatment rules may be disputed as warrants, and if so, they require backing. A justification involves showing both that the rule is *valid* and that it is *applicable* in the present case.[11] The following figure illustrates the full sequence of professional reasoning (for reasons of simplicity, the rebuttals, qualifiers, and backings have been omitted from the figure).[12]

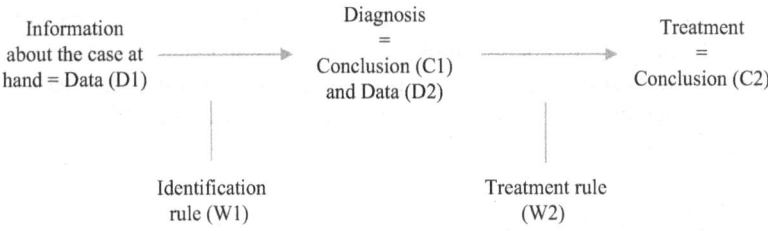

Warrants may have different degrees of force. The force of a strong warrant approaches the force of a rule of deduction: if the premises are true, the conclusion must be true. If all humans are mortal, and if John is a human, then John is mortal. The conclusion is entailed by the premises. A weak warrant mentions only those issues that ought to be considered in the process of reasoning, and it can be completely unspecific with regard to how they should be understood and considered. Discretion, as a form of reasoning, belongs to the part of this continuum where warrants are weakest. *In other words, discretionary reasoning comprises reasoning with weak warrants.* In the case of professional reasoning, it comprises reasoning with weak identification and treatment rules. This way of approaching discretionary reasoning achieves five things. *First*, by emphasizing the conditions under which one must reason (not the object of reasoning), one can see what is common in legal discretion and, for instance, in clinical judgment in medicine or in other kinds of professional judgments. However, there are some differences, which will be discussed below. *Second*, when the force of the warrants is the important variable, the borderline between discretionary reasoning and free fantasy is drawn by the presence of warrants. If no warrants govern reasoning, then it is not discretionary reasoning. *Third*, weak warrants explain some of the peculiar features of the exercise of discretion – for example, its similarity to the concept of bricolage put forward by Claude Lévi-Strauss.[13] A bricoleur is a craftsperson who repairs things with whatever is at hand. It is frequently like that in discretionary reasoning. One must often use what is at hand to arrive at a justified conclusion at all. This is probably also a part of the explanation why discretionary reasoning is often compared with intuition, special sensibilities, and so on. *Fourth*, this way of analyzing discretionary reasoning can provide clues for understanding both the role and the pitfalls of the heuristics studied in cognitive psychology. Heuristics can be seen as warrants, which over time have been selected because they often, under certain specific circumstances, give correct results. Many of the heuristics are, from a logical point of view, what we call identification rules. Logically speaking, heuristics are fallacious rules of inference. They are shortcuts that contain a grain of truth or are valid under certain circumstances, but not generally. *Finally*, this way of analyzing discretionary reasoning can sensitize us to one of the most problematic aspects of discretion. It is often in situations where discretionary reasoning is most urgently needed that it is most difficult to practice.

## Circumstances of discretion

The circumstances of discretion are the conditions under which discretionary reasoning is necessary so as to pass judgments about particular cases.[14] In other words, they are *sources of indeterminacy*. To illuminate the circumstances of discretion, we shall first take a look at legal rules. The basic form of a legal rule is as follows: *If x, then y*.[15] The antecedent $x$ classifies an action (or abstention) or a set of actions (or abstentions). The consequent $y$ describes the legal consequences of the antecedent's classification. Legal consequences do not emanate from an action itself but rather from its classification according to valid law. Under Norwegian criminal law, for example, someone who has committed a first-degree murder can be sentenced to up to twenty-one years in prison. Such a rule is intended to be strictly universal,

## The anatomy of discretion 29

namely, to be valid for all actions satisfying the conditions for first-degree murder that are specified in the antecedent. This is a characteristic feature of positive law. Universality is a way of materializing the principle of formal justice (or equal treatment). Legal rules are the strongest type of warrants there are in the realm of practical reasoning. Ideally, they should have a force that is similar to the force of the rules of deductive inference. However, in practice, this ideal cannot be achieved, mainly for two reasons. The first reason is that we do not have such strong warrants in inferences from descriptive premises (what the case is) to normative conclusions (what ought to be done). To a certain extent, legal rules mitigate the gap between the descriptive and the normative because their sortal terms are not purely descriptive. To classify someone's action as a murder is to say that this person has committed a crime. Thus, the inferences from premises to conclusion are not, strictly speaking, inferences from descriptive premises to normative conclusions. They are inferences from premises that describe normatively classified facts to normative conclusions. However, if legal consequences should follow from what someone has done, it is often not clear which consequences should follow. The second reason is that legal rules are not, and cannot be, purely formal. This characteristic distinguishes them from logical inference rules. Their application to concrete, particular cases demands that the antecedents be empirically true. If it is untrue that a person has committed a first-degree murder, then the sections about first-degree murder in criminal law do not apply to this person. In deduction, this is not so because it is purely formal. A logical inference can be valid even if its premises are false. Legal rules raise an empirical problem of applicability, which does not pertain to the purely formal rules of deductive inference. This is the problem of subsumption, which is essentially a problem of identification.

Strict subsumption is an ideal for legal rules that follows from the principles of the rule of law (mainly the principle of predictability of law enforcement). If a legal rule $L$ satisfies the criteria of strict subsumption, then for every action $A$ it must be possible to decide if $A$ is in accordance with or violates $L$ – that is, if $A$ is legal or not legal. In the ideal case, crimes should be precisely defined so that one could decide beyond doubt for every action whether it is a crime or not and what type of crime. If strict subsumption is unattainable, discretion must fill the gaps. There are at least three kinds of cases where legal rules have this form and where strict subsumption is nevertheless difficult or impossible to achieve. In the *first* kind of case, the antecedent (if $x$) is precise, but the consequent (then $y$) is not. It may be easy to decide which crime has been committed but difficult to decide its exact legal consequences. For example, the legal consequences of crime may be expressed as a variable (up to a certain number of years in prison) or may be dependent on the defendant's physical or mental fitness. In the *second* kind of case, the consequent is precise, but the antecedent is vague. It may, for example, be difficult to decide which crime has been committed because of a vague description of the crime; thus, that there are no clear rules of identification. The phenomenon to be classified may also be complex. In the *third* kind of case, both the antecedent and the consequent are vague. It can then be unclear if some action is covered by the law and what legal consequences follow if it is covered. Many cases in private law are like that. A judge, working much like an arbiter in this situation, has to listen to the parties, form an opinion about the facts, and take into consideration previous verdicts in similar cases while upholding certain general principles of reasonableness.

This way of understanding the circumstances of discretion applies not only to legal reasoning but also to medical diagnostics and treatment. In curative medicine (in contrast to much of preventive medicine), the aim is to reach conclusions about individual cases (i.e., to determine which diseases a patient has and how they can best be treated). Diagnoses and treatments are ideally connected as instrumental norms – or what Kant calls "hypothetical imperatives" – prescribing which means one should select to reach certain aims. If the patient has blocked blood vessels to the heart, then angioplasty or a bypass operation should be performed. The antecedent describes the diagnosis; the consequent describes the treatment. Hypothetical imperatives, like logical and legal rules of inference, have an if–then form. However, the thinking is quite different. Hypothetical imperatives should express confirmed empirical correlations or causal connections between activities (means) and desired states (ends). When hypothetical imperatives function as warrants in practical arguments, their force depends on how well the connection between means and ends is confirmed. With hypothetical imperatives – as with laws – there is a problem of subsumption. However, it has, unlike with laws, three parts rather than only two: the antecedent, the consequent, and the connection between them. In hypothetical imperatives, the connection between premises and conclusion is empirical rather than logical or normative. Because the problem of subsumption with hypothetical imperatives has three parts, there are at least *four* kinds of cases where strict subsumption is not possible. The first three cases have the same structure as in legal reasoning: the antecedent is precise, but the consequent is vague; the antecedent is vague, but the consequent is precise; or the antecedent and the consequent are both vague. The first kind covers cases in which an illness is easy to diagnose, but there is no uncontroversial standard treatment available. The second kind covers cases in which it is difficult to find a diagnosis here and now, but the treatment is relatively uncontroversial once the diagnosis is found. For example, if a physician has a patient with severe chest pains, but is two hours away from the emergency department, she will not have access to X-ray or blood samples, and EKG does not give certain answers. In this situation, should one transport all patients with chest pains to a hospital, or should one use clinical judgment to determine the borderline cases that must be transported to a hospital, even if there are no clear indications of cardiovascular disease?[16] The third type covers "uncertain illnesses," such as whiplash, fibromyalgia, and burnout syndrome. It also covers many mental illnesses. The fourth kind of case demonstrates an important difference between medicine and jurisprudence. When hypothetical imperatives function as warrants, their force depends on how well the connection between means and ends is corroborated. The connection between premises and conclusion contains an independent problem of subsumption, which is absent with legal rules where the connection is *stipulated*, not discovered. If someone commits a first-degree murder in Norway, that person should be convicted and imprisoned for up to twenty-one years. Conducting specific investigations to find out whether the connection between premises and conclusion is valid does not make sense here. If it is invalid, then the law is invalid; it does not mean that there is something empirically wrong with the connection. However, this is different in hypothetical imperatives. Here the connection between premises and conclusion must be justified *empirically*. The problem in medicine, like in other professions based on empirical knowledge, is that connections of this kind are justified statistically. There are rarely justified causal laws in the strict sense of the term.[17] Most – maybe the majority of – medical knowledge consists of aggregated data, from which, of course, one can also make well-founded assumptions about causality. However, one cannot draw unambiguous conclusions for individual cases from data on an aggregated level. Although a cure has a documented effect in 85 percent of cases, one cannot infer that it will also work in this case. The strict subsumption of individual cases under general laws is then unachievable. Thus, practitioners must use their clinical judgment to decide whether a certain means–end scheme, which can be well documented, can be actually applied to a particular patient.

## *Normative contexts of discretion*

As we have shown, discretionary reasoning is bounded by warrants, but warrants have different degrees of force. Discretion is found at that end of the continuum where the warrants are weak, and subsumption is found at the other end. In addition to this kind of boundedness, discretionary reasoning is bounded by specific sets of normative expectations. We shall call such sets of expectations the *normative contexts of discretion*. They do not function in the same way as warrants in practical arguments. Warrants justify the transition from premises to conclusion in particular cases. The normative contexts of discretion specify general requirements that activities – of which discretion is an unavoidable part – must satisfy. One of the problematic features of discretion as reasoning with weak warrants is that it creates an intrinsic tension with the normative expectations under which it works or a tension between different normative expectations.

With the help of some simple distinctions, one can differentiate between normative contexts: (1) between contexts that demand *comparative consistency* and those that require *individualization* and (2) between two kinds of comparative consistency: one is entailed by the principle of formal justice, or the principle of *equal treatment*; the other is entailed by the demand for *reproducibility*. Comparative consistency means that the same case is judged in an equal way by different persons, at different times, or in different situations. Thus, there are three ideal-typical normative contexts of discretion: (a) contexts where discretion is bounded by a requirement of comparative consistency entailed by the formal principle of justice, (b) contexts where discretion is bounded by a requirement of comparative consistency entailed by the principle of reproducibility, and (c) contexts where discretion is bounded by a requirement of individualization. Judicial discretion primarily belongs to the first kind of context. Clinical judgment primarily belongs to the second kind of context. Different kinds of care are primarily examples of the third kind of context. The contexts can also be mixed and collide with one another. An example of a mixed and nonperspicuous context of discretion is the street-level bureaucrats' distribution of benefits and services based on need.

*a) The formal principle of justice*

Judicial discretion is a prime example of discretion that labors under the constraints of the formal principle of justice (or equal treatment). The formal principle of justice demands comparative consistency in judgments across time, space, and persons (those who judge). However, there is an intrinsic tension between this principle and discretionary reasoning. Discretion has – because of weak warrants – an intrinsic propensity to threaten comparative consistency across time, space, and persons. It introduces a noneliminable element of variation. The same case can be judged differently at different times, in different situations, and by different persons – even if the case itself is unchanged and the reasoning is carried out in a competent, thorough, and conscientious manner. Numerous examples exist of how discretion can threaten comparative consistency. The marking of course papers in disciplines where there are no standard answers is just one example.

## b) The principle of reproducibility

Clinical judgments do not labor under the formal principle of equality. They are not bounded by precedents and will not become a precedent unless, of course, it enters legal contexts. However, a demand for comparative consistency also exists in clinical judgments. If a physician diagnoses a patient as having tuberculosis (TB) at $t_0$, then the physician should also diagnose the patient as having TB at $t_1$ if the patient has not been cured in the meantime. Other physicians should reach the same conclusion. If not, one of the diagnoses or both diagnoses must be wrong. This is important, among other things, because diagnoses follow patients through the health care system. However, what justifies this requirement of consistency is not the formal principle of equality but rather the demand that diagnoses be reproducible. This represents another kind of normative context. Reproducibility is also a normative expectation but is different from the principle of equal treatment.

Equal treatment is a way of expressing an idea of fairness between persons. Reproducibility expresses another idea: if a phenomenon cannot be reproduced, there are good reasons to believe that it is not real, namely, that it is caused by an error or is the product of someone's imagination or methods. Thus, the distinction between two ways of justifying the demands of comparative consistency creates a rough distinction between two kinds of normative contexts for discretion or between two ways in which discretion is bounded. The first kind of context is characterized by the fact that the formal principle of equality functions as a normative constraint by imposing a demand for comparative consistency. The second kind of context is characterized by another kind of normative framework, namely, reproducibility. Reproducibility also demands comparative consistency – but not for the same reason as equal treatment. The element of variation that discretion introduces can also threaten the conditions of consistency for clinical judgments in the same way that it can threaten the conditions of consistency for juridical discretion. There is an intrinsic tension between clinical judgments and their own normative context.

## c) The principle of individualization

When nurses consider how to comfort and care for their patients, or when teachers think about how to adapt teaching methods to their pupils' abilities, their reasoning is discretionary. They must find out what – everything considered – is best for their individual patients/pupils. They then reason within a normative context where it is required that treatment of individual patients/pupils takes into account their particularities. This can be called a requirement of individualization. Here we use nurses and teachers as examples, but the same kind of reasoning is often used by physicians or social workers and by other professionals. Patients, pupils, and clients can have needs that are special and specific to a particular situation. Therefore, the treatment of this person does not determine how one should relate to other persons, who, by virtue of their individuality, possess quite different needs. The considerations in question are not comparative. They express what is best for a unique person in a particular situation.

Individualization can be in tension with fairness considerations when scarce resources must be distributed among many needy persons. However, in contrast to the other two contexts, there is no intrinsic tension between discretion and comparative consistency. The intrinsic problem with individualization is what might be called *failed perfectionism*. Individualization without any demand for comparative consistency is a perfectionist ideal. It is, as such, limitless. If one has enough time, money, and energy, one can individualize as much as one wishes on the basis of thicker and thicker descriptions of the unique case, without ever reaching the perfect state. To avoid this, the demand for individualization is normally tied to some idea of what is a sufficient attainment of the aim of individualization, for example, to lessen a patient's suffering or improve a patient's physical, mental, or social functioning. However, the idea of a threshold does not halt individualization but rather triggers discretionary evaluations of what is needed in each case separately so as to reach the threshold.

### d) Mixed contexts

The contexts of discretion can be mixed, and the mixture can create problems in itself. One context may demand consistency in another, but discretion in this other context cannot deliver what the first context demands. Equal treatment may demand reproducibility, but it may not necessarily be achieved. The demands in one context may also undermine the demands in another. Individualization of care may result in unjustified unequal treatment, and concern for equal treatment may result in inefficient individualization – that is, relevant differences between cases are not taken properly into account.

A mixture of contexts occurs when professionals practicing discretion act as gatekeepers in the welfare state. They must determine which individuals are in need and entitled to certain benefits and to what they are entitled. Let us illustrate with the requirements for receiving a disability pension in Norway.[18] The process of obtaining a disability pension requires discretion about legal facts but not about legal consequences. If someone is classified as disabled, the legal consequence – that is, what this person has a right to – is clear. However, who is considered disabled?

Assume that someone suffers from an "uncertain" illness. A physician is tasked with performing diagnostics and prognostics in a legal framework to assess whether this person is eligible to receive a disability pension. The result of the clinical examination should not only be reproducible but also enter into a legal process – in the sense that it can become a precedent or, conversely, that it can be appealed. It is then subjected to two kinds of requirements for comparative consistency. One is justified by the principle of formal justice. The other is justified by the demand for reproducibility. Because of the necessity of making comparisons with other cases, the law demands a clear judgment about the person's future capability of earning enough for a decent living. If the judgment is unclear, arbitrariness in the treatment of different persons with similar complaints may be the result. However, the physician may be unable to make an unambiguous judgment in this case. Uncertain illnesses do not sit well with the demand for reproducibility. The law then demands something that cannot be provided in this case. Reproducibility is not achieved, and tension with the principle of formal justice is also created. Other patients examined by other physicians may receive what this patient does not receive, even if the cases are rather similar.

This example shows how discretion is bounded by normative contexts. The formal principle of justice demands comparative consistency because cases that cannot be distinguished normatively must be treated equally. Unequal treatment demands relevant differences. Arguments in such a discussion have to establish normatively relevant similarities or differences between cases. Reproducibility demands comparative consistency because one has reason to think that irreproducible phenomena may be the product of the researcher's or the clinician's imagination or methods. Arguments in such a discussion should make it plausible to think that something does or does not exist. So, even if comparative consistency is crucial in both contexts, different kinds of arguments are required. This is also the case if individualization is compared with the demand for comparative consistency. Arguments in a context of individualization should establish what is special or unique about someone's needs or situation. A comparison of cases then has no place, except in the sense that it is needed to establish uniqueness. The principle is to follow the individual's preferences or one's own evaluation of what is best for the individual, independently of what is good for others.

The principle of individualization can be defended in terms of justice, that is, as a way of giving individuals what they are each owed. What is someone's due is determined in relation to some fixed standard, not in relation to others. If the concern is that everyone reaches a certain level of something, then interpersonal comparisons are not necessary. The standard is noncomparative and so is the meaning of giving each his due.[19] However, because individuals need different things, different efforts, and different amounts of resources to achieve an adequate level of something, there is an unavoidable trade-off between noncomparative considerations and concerns about interpersonal, comparative fairness.

## *Burdens of discretion and heuristics*

Everything that can influence the *results* of discretionary reasoning (i.e., discretionary judgments) is relevant to an explanation of why there are inherent tensions between discretionary reasoning and demands for comparative consistency. For this reason, we must distinguish among at least three kinds of factors that can influence discretionary judgments:

1. One kind of factors are unavoidable and influence the use of theoretical and practical reasoning per se. Such factors would also pertain to ideal reasoners – that is, individuals who engage in reasoning under ideal conditions. To be an ideal reasoner is to commit no logical or inferential errors. However, making no logical or inferential errors does not exclude some other kinds of influential sources of variation, for instance, conceptual vagueness, which cannot, in principle, be completely eradicated.
2. Another kind of influences stem from the fact that humans are nonideal reasoners – that is, individuals who encounter difficulties with handling information and make mistakes in their reasoning. Individuals do commit logical and inferential errors, often without being aware of committing them, especially when they are engaged in identifying phenomena or assessing the likelihood of future events. Some of these inferential errors even seem to be an important part of the mental makeup of individuals because they use different kinds of heuristics to reach conclusions, for instance, about what is likely to happen in the future.
3. Moreover, there are sloppy and bad reasoning. However, we are not interested here in negligence as a factor that may influence discretionary judgments, even though it can be – and probably is – an important factor.

The borders separating these three kinds of factors are not impermeable, but they are sufficiently tight for our purposes.

IDEAL REASONERS: BURDENS OF DISCRETION

It is a feature of discretionary reasoning (and of practical reasoning as such along the whole continuum) that even persons who reason as thoroughly and conscientiously as possible can reach different conclusions. Reasonable disagreement among reasonable persons must be expected because discretionary reasoning contains sources of variation in conclusions. There are sources of variation that are inherent in discretion as a form of reasoning (and in practical reasoning as such) and that are as original as the circumstances requiring it. Modifying an expression from John Rawls, we call these sources of variation the burdens of discretion.[20] Rawls' discussion is premised on the assumption that reasoners commit no logical errors, so we are talking about ideal reasoners. The following phenomena belong to the burdens of discretion (the list is most likely only a partial one, and thus, more phenomena could be added to it):

1   Discretionary reasoning is to a large extent *casuistic*. In contrast to subsumption, casuistry applies analogical reasoning. Analogical reasoning is based on assessments of concrete similarities and differences.[21] To justify a conclusion about what one ought to do in a case, one investigates *if, in what sense*, and *to what degree* it is similar to or different from other cases where conclusions have already been reached. This is the basic principle of casuistry: concrete similarities or differences to other cases codetermine the judgments in the present case. This is also the basic principle of case or common law, which is essentially casuistic. Casuistry is so important in discretionary reasoning for two reasons. One reason has to do with the role of warrants. The other reason has to do with the role of normative contexts. In reasoning with weak warrants, one must assess concrete similarities and differences, not only when justifying descriptions of situations, but also when inferring action consequences. Actually, the only accessible warrant may be the demand that similar cases be treated equally, and different cases unequally. The other reason why casuistry is important is that it is the only way to satisfy the requirements of comparative consistency when subsumption is impossible. One must then establish concrete similarities or differences between single particular cases. The requirements of comparative consistency can be satisfied as a side effect if judgments about concrete similarities and differences converge across situations, times, or persons.
    However, analogy is intransitive. The fact that $A$ is analogous to $B$, and $B$ to $C$, does not entail that $C$ is analogous to $A$. Analogies are intransitive because they express similarity, which is also intransitive. Identity, by contrast, is transitive: if $A$ is identical to $B$, and $B$ is identical to $C$, then $C$ is identical to $A$. The intransitivity of analogies explains many cases of inconsistent assessments over time. When the decision about $C$ is made by reference to decisions about previous cases, the similarity between the earliest cases and $C$ can be very slim indeed. In part, intransitivity can be counteracted by treating the first decision

in a chain as a paradigm, precedent, or reference case. A chain of divergent assessments is then closed or prevented from being established. However, memory is fallible, and the details in the first case can be easily forgotten. The reference case then becomes a precedent as it is now remembered, not as it originally was.

The intransitivity of analogies explains why the casuistic features of discretionary reasoning are in tension with the requirements of comparative consistency. It may even apply to discretionary reasoning that is carried out thoroughly and conscientiously.

2. The *indeterminacy of descriptions* is a second source of variation. The distribution of benefits based on need often demands complex descriptions of particular cases. Different kinds of professionals – physicians, nurses, social workers, lawyers, and others – often contribute to such descriptions. They have their own specific professional vocabularies, which need not be well calibrated to one another. Diagnostics and legal decisions more generally also demand complex descriptions. Cases must always be compared under specific descriptions, which specify the sense in which they are similar or different. Descriptions can be indeterminate and controversial, as well as dependent on the abilities of professionals and clients to articulate what they want and how they evaluate things. Descriptions are often not only purely descriptive but also have normative content (i.e., they contain moral, legal, and political elements). However, there is no clear answer to the question of when a description is complete or sufficiently rich. There are no unambiguous cutoff points in such matters. There is also no clear answer to the question of when the phenomena being compared are similar or different. One can – in a certain sense – make a description as thick as one wants; nevertheless, it does not create an unambiguous cutoff point in the determination of similarity and difference. The only guideline for composing descriptions is often a list of factors relevant to discretionary judgments. However, such a list normally provides only pegs, not criteria, for when the description is sufficiently rich or complete. Criteria may, moreover, be embedded in local traditions and cultures of the workplaces of physicians, social workers, and other professionals. Local traditions and cultures can vary considerably. The indeterminacy of descriptions opens up the possibility for the influence of local traditions and cultures, which can vary and exercise considerable influence on how discretionary reasoning is practiced – even if those who reason, commit no logical errors or fallacious inferences.

3. An unavoidable element in discretionary reasoning is *firsthand experience*. Discretionary reasoning may be exercised in a highly conscientious way, and all relevant factors may be considered. Nevertheless, it is

reasoning under circumstances where there are no clear rules, or where rules may leave loopholes open, or where rules may have to be ranked without clear criteria of priority. Under such circumstances, firsthand experiences – or what Michael Polanyi "personal knowledge" – play an important role in reaching conclusions.[22] Arguments in favor of discretion often regard this kind of knowledge not only as unavoidable in exercising discretion but also as its hallmark. Discretion is compared with *phronesis* (practical wisdom), which, according to Aristotle, only experienced persons can have.[23] There is some truth in this claim, but firsthand experience is not only an asset.

Two points must be emphasized about firsthand experiences as a source of variation in discretionary reasoning. There is a difference between those who have a great deal of relevant experience and those who do not. People have more or less relevant experience, and this experience can influence judgments. For this reason, an important difference may exist between experienced and not-so-experienced reasoners. Firsthand experiences are, in addition, always made by concrete, particular persons in concrete, particular situations. They will vary between persons because different lives take different paths, with some paths never crossing. Professional careers also take different paths. In reasoning where firsthand experiences play a role, particular persons cannot fully replace one another. One cannot replace *A* with *B* and expect to get exactly the same thing. One can only reasonably expect to get something more or less similar. If a teacher is replaced with another teacher, one gets something similar, but not identical, to that which one had.

4   According to Rawls, there are certain noneliminable hazards that influence both theoretical and practical reasoning. He calls them the "burdens of judgment."[24] Reason, both theoretical and practical, works under conditions implying that agreement is difficult to reach even if those judging are fully reasonable. That is, disagreement is not caused by "prejudice and bias, self- and group interest, blindness and willfulness."

Although we have already touched on some of the phenomena on Rawls' list, the entire list is of interest because it considers some of the aforementioned sources of variation from a different perspective, namely, the conditions of consensus and dissent. Rawls' list contains six points, which we here present in a somewhat simplified form:

a) Relevant facts in a case can be complex, contradictory, and difficult to assess because they point in different directions.

b) Even if there is agreement about which considerations are relevant in a case, there can be disagreement about their weight, and therefore, different conclusions can be drawn.

c)  All concepts are to a certain degree indeterminate and vulnerable to hard cases. The use of concepts must therefore be based on judgments and interpretation, wherein reasonable persons can disagree.

d)  The experiences that one has had during one's life shape how one selects facts and how one weighs moral and political values. In modern societies with many different positions, many ethnically and socially diverse groups, and many kinds of division of labor, people's experiences are varied enough so as to make assessments different, at least in cases with some complexity.

e)  Most often there are normative considerations with different forces on all sides of a case; hence, an overall assessment of these considerations can be difficult.

f)  One cannot realize all possible positive values simultaneously. For this reason, one must range values that per se can be equally good. However, there is mostly a lack of clear and uncontroversial criteria for such rankings.

These cognitive factors are sources of variation in discretionary reasoning. Hence, individual $A$ and individual $B$ may judge the same case differently. Although their disagreement is reasonable, it nevertheless creates a tension with comparative consistency.

When we claim that the burdens of discretion to a large degree explain tensions between discretionary reasoning and comparative consistency, it is important to be precise about what that means. First, as already mentioned, it does not imply that discretionary reasoning is normally carried out in a sloppy manner. The burdens of discretion can influence discretionary reasoning and create tensions between discretionary reasoning and the demands of comparative consistency, even if discretionary reasoning is carried out in the most informed, conscious, thorough, and conscientious manner possible. It is inherent in discretion as a kind of reasoning that requirements of comparative consistency can be difficult to satisfy. Discretionary reasoning is a kind of reasoning that always labors under certain conditions that are unavoidable sources of variation.

Second, nor does it mean that discretionary reasoning is never carried out in a bad and sloppy manner. There exists, of course, a great deal of sloppy discretionary reasoning, which can also create difficulties with regard to comparative consistency. However, these are not difficulties in principle, and they can be overcome by correcting sloppy reasoning. The burdens of discretion, by contrast, create difficulties of another kind.

Third, how the burdens of discretion influence the results of discretionary reasoning can depend on the circumstances of discretion. Even if discretionary reasoning is reasoning with weak warrants, the force of the warrants can be different.

## NONIDEAL REASONERS: HEURISTICS AND COGNITIVE BIASES

During the past thirty to forty years, a great deal of evidence has been compiled (for instance, through experimental research in cognitive psychology and the psychology of decisions) supporting the claim that humans rely heavily on heuristics, or mental shortcuts.[25] According to psychologists, the mind has two systems: one system is fast and intuitive (System 1), and the other system is slow and analytical (System 2). The use of heuristics is characteristic of System 1. Heuristics are simple procedures for answering difficult questions by replacing them with less difficult ones. They can be "fast and frugal" ways of reaching a conclusion, for example, about what something is or about how frequent it is.[26] They usually hit the target; however, they do not hit the target in every case, and they create systematic biases in our thinking. Logically, they are fallacious inference rules because one cannot conclude from the fact that a rule hits the target in most cases (or in all cases up to now) that it will hit the target in all cases. Heuristics overgeneralize, but as long as the factors they pick out for identifying something are sufficiently closely associated with the correct identity, they are useful inference rules. However, they may lead one astray, especially when one is ignorant of them. Indeed, one is often very conscious about some of the rules of thumb being used and aware that they are only roughly correct (i.e., not completely correct). For this reason, precautions are taken when using them. This is not so with heuristics. They are, so to speak, rules of thumb on which one constantly relies, without being aware of the fact that one does so.

According to our analysis of discretionary reasoning, heuristics can be considered *kinds of warrants* – that is, general inference rules that bridge the gap between data and conclusions, for instance, about what something is or the likelihood of uncertain future events. Heuristics are, however, different from the burdens of discretion, which, in principle, can be corrected or counteracted. Even when they are known, heuristics are difficult to correct and counteract. They are situated, so to speak, very deep in one's mental makeup or in one's way of processing information.

In a seminal article, Daniel Kahneman and Amos Tversky identify three, now considered canonical, heuristics and some of the cognitive biases to which they can lead.[27] The first of these heuristics is the *representativeness heuristic*. Kahneman and Tversky note the following:

> Many of the probabilistic questions with which people are concerned belong to one of the following types: what is the probability that object A belongs to class B? What is the probability that event A originates from process B? What is the probability that process B will generate event A? In answering such questions, people typically rely on the representativeness heuristic, in which probabilities are evaluated by the

degree to which A is representative of B, that is, by the degree to which A resembles B. For example, when A is highly representative of B, the probability that A originates from B is judged to be high.[28]

A famous demonstration of how biases can creep in when using this heuristic is the Linda experiment. Subjects were told that "Linda is thirty-one years old, single, outspoken, and very bright. She majored in philosophy. As a student, she was deeply concerned with issues of discrimination and social justice, and also participated in anti-nuclear demonstrations." When asked about what is more likely, that Linda is "a bank teller" or "a bank teller and is active in the feminist movement," about 85 to 90 percent of undergraduates at several major American universities chose the second option. The explanation for this obvious mistake (all feminist bank tellers are bank tellers) is that Linda seems to match the latter option better than the former.[29] Another and more drastic demonstration is the experiment that David Eddy carried out with one hundred physicians about the probability of breast cancer. They were presented with the following case:

> A physician has encountered a slight lump in a woman's breast. He thinks there is a 1 percent probability that the patient has breast cancer. If the woman *does* have breast cancer, then there is an 80 percent probability that mammography will detect this (she tests positive). If she *does not* have cancer, there is still a 10 percent probability that she tests positive. What is the probability that a woman who tests positive has breast cancer?

Ninety-five of one hundred physicians answered that the probability was between 70 and 80 percent. The correct answer is 7.5 percent. It seems that the physicians made use of the representativeness heuristic and replaced the difficult probability question with a simpler one: how typical or representative is it that women who have breast cancer test positive?[30]

According to our scheme, the representativeness heuristic will then function as a rule of identification, thereby contributing to answering the following question: what is $A$? However, how does one, based on the fact that $A$ resembles $B$, conclude that $A$ belongs to the class of $B$? An inference rule (a *warrant* in Toulmin's terminology) is needed. A possible inference could resemble the following one ($D$ is the datum, $C$ is the conclusion, and $W$ is the warrant):

D --------------------------------------------------- C

A strongly resembles B                A is a B

W

If an X strongly resembles Y, the probability that X is a Y is high.

In many cases this will work very well. It works well when there is a match between representativeness and objective probabilities. Assume that one is presented with $A$ and that $A$ strongly resembles $B$. One judges the probability of $A$ being a $B$ and not a $C$ on the basis of the fact that $A$ resembles $B$ much more than it resembles $C$. This can also be formulated as a rule of inference, which can function as a tacit warrant for claims about what $A$ is: if $A$ resembles $B$ more than $C$, then infer that $A$ is a $B$. If the ratio $C$:$B$ in the world is 1:99, then the objective probability that $A$ is actually a $B$ and not a $C$ is very high, and the heuristic will on average be very useful and hit the target. It will be useful when it is simultaneously true that $A$ resembles $B$ more than $C$ and that there are many more $B$s than $C$s in the world. However, the ratio $C$:$B$ can be much lower in many situations. The heuristic can then lead to severe and systematic errors, simply because representativeness is affected by factors other than objective probabilities. Representativeness can be affected by superficial resemblances, which actually reveal nothing about objective probabilities, but objective probabilities do not affect representativeness.

The second heuristic is the *availability heuristic*. Kahneman and Tversky provide an example to describe it:

> There are situations in which people assess the frequency of a class or the probability of an event by the ease with which instances or occurrences can be brought to mind. For instance, one may assess the risk of heart attack among middle-aged people by recalling such occurrences among one's acquaintances.[31]

If many of one's acquaintances have had a heart attack, one can judge the risk to be high. If few among one's acquaintances have had a heart attack, one can judge the risk to be low. Hence, availability is used as a proxy for frequency. However, the fact that heart attacks among one's acquaintances are easily remembered does not imply that one's acquaintances form a representative sample of the population. One will therefore probably misjudge the risk of having a heart attack.

The availability heuristic also works well in many cases, mainly because instances of large classes are usually recalled faster and better than instances of less frequent classes. This is probably so because one is more familiar and has more experiences with members of large classes. One encounters them more often. Therefore, when they are believed to be frequent, they are probably also frequent in reality. The prevalence of normal pneumonia is a great deal higher than the prevalence of Ebola. If one assesses the risk of contracting pneumonia from its remembered prevalence among one's acquaintances, the chances of being right are a great deal higher than the chances of being right if one assesses the risk of contracting Ebola on the basis of its remembered prevalence among one's acquaintances. Thus, in many kinds of situations, there will be a match between availability and objective probabilities. However, in other situations, the availability heuristic can lead to severe and systematic errors because availability is affected by factors other than objective probabilities, for instance, how easy it is to remember things.

The third heuristic identified by Kahneman and Tversky is the *heuristic of adjustment and anchoring*. Kahneman and Tversky note that

> [i]n many situations, people make estimates by starting from an initial value that is adjusted to yield the final answer. The initial value, or starting point, may be suggested by the formulation of the problem, or it may be the result of a partial computation. ... That is, different starting points yield different estimates, which are biased toward the initial values.[32]

In an experiment, Kahneman and Tversky asked students to write down the number on which a wheel of fortune stopped. The wheel was rigged so that it always stopped on either ten or sixty-five. They then asked the students to state the percentage of African nations in the United Nations. On average, those who had seen the number ten answered 25 percent, and those who had seen the number sixty-five answered 45 percent.[33] The anchoring effect can be described as a kind of tunnel vision. The initial formulation of a problem "locks" the search for solutions in one direction and excludes other directions. One reason is that anchoring can result in the premature closure of investigations and examinations. If investigations and examinations are not closed, they will still be skewed the whole time in one direction.

Heuristics seem to be pervasive and a very important kind of warrant in human reasoning about what something is and about the future likelihood of uncertain events. Physicians must form beliefs about what kind of disease is indicated by a set of symptoms. They must also form beliefs about how likely it is that a certain treatment will be efficacious. Social workers must form beliefs about how likely it is that a certain intervention will work best for their clients. Belief formation about what phenomena are and to which classes they belong as well as about uncertain future events thus belongs at the core of professional discretion. The cognitive biases that heuristics create also seem to be major causal factors behind professional errors, for instance, diagnostic errors in medicine.[34] There is no prima facie good reason to assume that this is different in other kinds of professional decisions or in any other kind of discretionary reasoning.

## Concluding remarks

Understood in epistemic terms, discretion is a form of practical reasoning – the aim being to draw conclusions about what ought to be done in particular cases – where warrants are weak. There are intrinsic tensions between this kind of reasoning and the demands of comparative consistency which can be explained by the burdens of discretion. Discretionary reasoning may also rely on heuristics that bias judgments. For these reasons this kind of reasoning represents a normative problem at the core of welfare states. We have not devoted space to sloppy discretionary judgments because carelessness does not belong to discretionary reasoning as such, while the burdens of discretion as well as the use of heuristics do. Moreover, it is easier to do something about sloppy discretion. The most drastic measure is to fire those who are sloppy. It is much more difficult to do something drastic with the burdens of discretion and heuristics, without abolishing discretionary reasoning itself. Discretionary reasoning is reasoning with weak warrants, and there is not much that can be done about that. With regard to the burdens of discretion and heuristics, it is important to become conscious of them so that one can understand why persons, who are not careless, nevertheless, can reach different conclusions about a case and make cognitive errors. Becoming conscious is the first step, but it need not be the last step as we will attempt to show in Chapter 4, where we outline a set of accountability mechanisms.

## Notes

1 Alexy (2002, 393).
2 Dworkin (1977, 31).
3 Dworkin (1977, 32).
4 This is an oblique reference to John Rawls' (1955/1999) famous article "Two Concepts of Rules."
5 Habermas (1996, 120).
6 Montesquieu (1949, 159) states that "judges are no more than the mouth that pronounces the words of the law, mere passive beings, incapable of moderating either its force or rigour."
7 According to Goodin (1988, 193), if individuals have *complete* discretion, they are under no obligation to justify their decisions, either to others or to themselves.
8 On this point, see Wellmer (1993, 39) and Günther (2008, sec. III).
9 On practical reasoning, see, for example, Gauthier (1963) and Habermas (1994).
10 Toulmin (1958) and Alexy (1983, 3.3.3).
11 See Günther (1988).
12 This figure is taken from Wallander and Molander (2014, 2016).
13 Lévi-Strauss (1966, 21).
14 This concept is inspired by the Rawls' (1971, §22) concept "circumstances of justice." These circumstances refer to the conditions of social cooperation that give rise to questions of justice.
15 Koller (1997, II:2).
16 We owe this example to Anne Kveim Lie.
17 Hempel (1970).
18 Individuals are eligible for disability benefits if their earning ability is permanently impaired by at least 50 percent owing to illness, injury, or defect.

19 See Feinberg (1974).
20 Rawls (1993, lecture II, 53). "The burdens of judgment" proper are presented as point 4. Points 1 to 3 are put together by us, not by Rawls. Rawls' issue was not discretionary reasoning but rather reasonable disagreement among reasonable persons.
21 Sunstein (1993).
22 Polanyi (1958).
23 Aristotle (1976, Book 6, V).
24 Rawls (1993, lecture II, §2).
25 See note 51.
26 Girgenzer (2004).
27 Kahneman and Tversky (1974).
28 Kahneman and Tversky (1974, 36).
29 Kahneman (2011, chap. 15).
30 Kirkebøen (2009). Eddy's experiment is reported in Eddy (1982).
31 Kahneman and Tversky (1974, 42–43).
32 Kahneman and Tversky (1974, 46).
33 Kahneman (2011, 119).
34 Groopman (2007).

# 3 Professional discretion in the welfare state

Two normative tensions

In providing for basic needs as a *matter of right*, the welfare state introduces a new category of legal positions and relations compared with the constitutional state (*Rechtsstaat*) and the democratic state.[1] Welfare rights are positive rights that oblige the state to provide individuals with something they cannot obtain through market transactions, owing to a lack of financial means or an insufficient market supply.[2] Because these rights mean an expansion of law into new areas, and a more detailed legal regulation of formerly legally regulated areas, they have been associated with a trend toward juridification.[3] However, juridification processes in the welfare state vary from stronger to weaker legal regulation, from stronger to weaker rights to benefits and services. In some areas, the rules that specify who is entitled to what are clear; in others, they are more or less discretionary. When juridification takes the latter form, discretionary power is conferred to diverse groups of professionals whose judgments about needs and circumstances mediate claims: one has a right to something under relatively vague rules applied by nonlegal professionals, for example, social workers and doctors.[4] The scope for discretion is increased when the task is not to administer rights but to realize certain goals or states through public intervention (i.e., to find the adequate means to reach a prescribed end). Sometimes rights are linked to purposes, as when Norwegian welfare law regards social assistance as both a right (given certain circumstances) and as a means to enable the receiver to become self-sufficient.[5] During the last decades so-called activation policies have been a central component in welfare reforms across OECD countries. These policies make rights to benefits conditional on active job search and participation in training programs and other work-related activities.[6] One probable implication of increasing conditionality of welfare benefits is more extensive use of discretion in welfare systems.[7]

In an influential account of juridification, Jürgen Habermas describes welfare state regulations as inherently ambivalent. On the one hand, they protect citizens against different types of risks and contribute to their social freedom; on the other hand, these regulations induce a "colonialization of the life-world." Habermas ascribes this ambivalence to "the structure of formal law," which "dictates the formulation of welfare-state guarantees as individual entitlements under precisely specified general legal conditions." To be subsumed under the law and dealt with administratively, situations "embedded in the context of a life history and of a concrete form of life" must be "subjected to violent abstraction."[8] However, as Ingeborg Maus points out, the danger of an "administrative penetration of the lifeworld"[9] is greatest in that part of the welfare system where the if–then structure of formal law is weakest – that is, where rules are vague and open-ended. A clear example is childcare interventions in "the best interests of the child."

In this chapter, we shall first take a closer look at the role of professional discretion in the welfare state and then approach it from the perspective of the democratic *Rechtsstaat*. We argue that there are unavoidable tensions between discretion and the requirements of the rule of law on the one hand, and between discretion and democratic authority on the other.

## Rights and discretion

Logically, the formulation of a right has three parts: (a) a description of or reference to the holder of the right, (b) a description of or reference to the holder(s) of the corresponding duties, and (c) an entitlement clause, which specifies the content to which the right holder has a legitimate claim and the duty bearer is obliged to provide. These features can be put into the formula: If $a$ has a right to $X$ against $b$, then $b$ has an obligation to $X$ against $a$.[10]

Like civil and political rights, social rights are equal rights, encompassing all citizens,[11] but in contrast to the former types of rights, they refer to phases of life, specific life conditions, and bad brute luck. Their justification is in terms of needs – that is, people suffer harm owing to the lack of something. Thus, an element of recognition of difference is also built into universal social rights. Old people are granted old age pensions not because of their age per se but rather because there is a connection between age, physical and mental capacities, and the ability to support oneself.

Social rights raise difficult questions about distributive justice. Which needs are of such importance that it is a public obligation to support them as a matter of right and, hence, an obligation of citizens to finance the support as taxpayers? When resources are scarce, and when welfare claims compete with one another and with other commitments and considerations, how should one prioritize? To what extent should individuals be held responsible for their situation, that is, to what extent can it be seen as a result of their own choices or of circumstances beyond their control? We have to ignore questions such as these here and instead focus on the formal structure of social rights – that is, to what extent they give space for professional discretion. However, this does not mean that political questions are irrelevant in connection with discretion. As we will see, one problematic aspect of discretion is that attitudes among professionals to the rights they are set to administer may influence how they judge in their administration of them.

Social rights are often vague in their formulation. It can be difficult to determine who satisfies the eligibility criteria. Discretion must be used to determine who is and who is not eligible in such cases. Moreover, some social rights have weakly specified entitlement clauses. It is not clear to what one is entitled when one has a right to $X$. Hence, it is not clear to what public institutions have a duty when they have a duty to provide $X$. When a right's entitlement clause is weakly specified, discretion must be used to determine exactly what public institutions have a duty to provide and to what the right holder is entitled.

We can distinguish at least three types of social rights:

1. There are rights that grant the same welfare benefit to everybody who is eligible to a certain status. An example is the old age pension, which everybody in Norway, for instance, receives at the age of sixty-seven years. Rights of this type are universal and unconditional and do not involve the use of discretion.
2. There are rights that grant the same welfare benefit to everybody who is eligible to claim a specific status, as determined by their situation. An example is the disability pension. For example, under the Norwegian Security Act, individuals are eligible to receive a disability benefit if their earning ability is permanently impaired by at least 50 percent owing to illness, injury, or defect. A great deal of discretion may be involved in determining whether someone is eligible. However, once this has been determined, it is clear to what the person is entitled.
3. There are rights that grant differentiated welfare benefits and services to individuals who are eligible to claim a certain status. With regard to the first two kinds of social rights listed here, it is clear what somebody who is eligible to claim a certain status is entitled to receive. In this case, however, what eligible persons are entitled to receive may differ based on need. For example, in the case of social assistance, a great deal of discretion may be involved both in deciding who should receive it and to what they are entitled. The Norwegian Social Services Act, for example, states that those who are "unable to support themselves by working or exercising financial rights are entitled to financial support" and that this support "should aim at making the person self-supporting." Moreover, conditions can be stipulated for the granting

of financial support," including "that the recipient shall be employed in suitable tasks in his or her municipality of residence for as long as the financial support is received."[12] Another clear example of a right that is discretionary with regard to both facts (who) and consequences (what) is the right to special education according to the Norwegian Education Act. The act states the following: "Pupils who either do not or are *unable to benefit satisfactorily* from ordinary tuition have the right to special education. In assessing what kind of tuition shall be provided, particular emphasis shall be placed on the pupil's *developmental prospects*. The content of the courses offered shall be such that the pupil receives *adequate benefit* from the tuition as a whole *in relation to other pupils and in relation to educational objectives that are realistic for the pupil*. Pupils who receive special education shall have the same total number of teaching hours as other pupils."[13] This right is discretionary all the way down. To emphasize the discretionary terms related to the determination of whom and of what, we added italics to the excerpt from the Norwegian Act. The only thing that is determinate in the enactment is the number of teaching hours.

Thus, there are some social rights that require little or no discretion both in determining who is entitled to them and to what they are then entitled. Some social rights require discretion in identifying who is entitled to them but not in determining what those rights are for the individuals who are entitled to them. Other social rights require discretion both in determining who are entitled to them and to what they are then entitled.

The stronger the discretionary element, the more difficult it is to enforce rights because it is not clear what should count as a violation of them. What should count as a violation becomes itself a discretionary issue. Another consequence of the discretionary element in rights is that they do not take certain issues off the political agenda and close political controversies. Instead, discretionary rights can contain political agendas in the entitlement clauses because the content of the entitlements is a matter of discretionary reasoning. Thus, a strong discretionary element reduces the extent to which rights can trump other (e.g., budgetary) considerations.

Let us return to professionals as street-level bureaucrats. To them, social rights function as allocation rules with the following if–then structure, as described by Goodin:

*Rule R*: If some individual $I$, who satisfies certain background conditions $B$, displays characteristics $K$ in circumstances $C$, then an individual $O$, who occupies official position $P$, should do $T$ to or for individual $I$.[14]

Within this structure, $K$ refers to the personal characteristics of the claimant (e.g., age, disease, disability), $C$ to the claimant's various nonpersonal circumstances (e.g., unemployment, parental responsibility, housing situation), and $B$ to the background conditions that the claimant needs to meet (e.g., citizenship, residency, payments). The treatment $T$ refers to providing (or not providing) a legally entrenched entitlement. The less determinate the eligibility criteria and entitlement clauses, the more space there is for discretion.

To eliminate discretion, one has to formulate clearer rules regarding who is entitled to what and design efficient review mechanisms. However, for many of the rights to receive benefits, and especially to receive services, it is simply not possible to specify general rules in such a way that entitlement in particular cases can be a matter of subsumption. It has also been argued that discretion serves a good end, namely, *individualized treatment*.[15] It ensures proper examination and treatment of individual cases because it permits professionals to consider what is particular and unique. Different persons may have different needs; thus, discretionary reasoning is necessary for flexible and individualized treatment. At the same time, the use of discretion is troublesome from legal as well as democratic points of view. To illustrate the trouble associated with discretion, we shall have a look at a vignette study on Norwegian general practitioners (GPs) assessment of "applicants" eligibility to receive disability pensions.[16]

## A case study: GPs and disability pensions

In this case study,[17] 360 GPs were asked to assess whether two "applicants" (presented as vignettes) satisfied the medical eligibility criteria for disability pension. The fictitious applicants in the study suffered from unexplained diseases, such as whiplash, musculoskeletal-related pain, and mental problems. In such cases, there are no clear-cut clinical findings and causal explanations; nevertheless, GPs must reach a justified conclusion based on their best judgment.

For patients to be eligible to receive a disability pension under the Norwegian social security system, a GP must confirm their illness or medical condition, provide a "valid" diagnosis of the illness or medical condition, and assess whether their capacity to earn a future living has been permanently reduced by at least 50 percent. The GP must also assess whether sufficient medical treatment and vocational rehabilitation have been tried. The Social Security Act is based on the presumption that GPs can give an objective and impartial account of the cases at hand, and assumes a causal relationship between claimants' diseases, the severity of their impairments, and the permanency of the reduction of their earning capacity.

The Norwegian study revealed three interesting findings. First, the assessments revealed great variation. Four of ten GPs concluded that the first applicant fulfilled the eligibility criteria, whereas three of ten GPs came to the opposite conclusion. For the second applicant, the results were reversed. For both applicants, three of ten GPs were unable to answer yes or no owing to uncertainty. Second, an examination of the GPs' comments on and justifications for their decisions showed a great deal of variation in their interpretation and understanding of identical information in the two vignettes. Third, an analysis revealed that the variations in judgments were correlated with indicators of the GPs' personal attitudes. The stronger a GP's expressed skepticism toward the disability pension system, the more restrictive the GP's interpretation of the medical eligibility criteria.

The case study, although not a naturalistic real-life study, neatly illustrates judgmental variation among medical professionals given the same information. Nevertheless, it is a plausible assumption that if the stories had been real-life stories, the more or less identical cases would have received different types of treatment. Moreover, it is a plausible assumption that the factors leading to different types of treatment would have included personal views, which do not belong on the checklist of considerations that is authorized when professionals are charged with making decisions of this kind.

## Two normative tensions

In democratic states, discretionary powers either are politically delegated or are amassed outside any process of democratic political delegation. They are either de jure or de facto discretionary powers.[18] De facto discretionary powers can be amassed as a matter of practical necessity, for example, to reduce decisional overload, and they are more or less tacitly accepted or tolerated or simply not noticed at all (or not recognized for what they actually are). Therefore, they are more difficult to bring under democratic control than de jure discretionary powers.

Typically, the discretionary powers enjoyed by welfare state professionals are a mixture of de jure powers and de facto powers. They are authorized to make certain kinds of decisions based on their best judgment; that is, they have formal mandates, which are normally restricted to carrying out certain tasks in certain ways. However, they often make – and must make – a great deal more decisions based on their best judgment than they are formally authorized to do. One may say that they also have informal mandates, consisting of all those things not covered by formal mandates that they must do to carry out their formally authorized work in a satisfactory manner or to support the work of other professionals.

The delegation of discretionary power to professionals that occupy official positions is troublesome from a political point of view for two sets of reasons. First, there is a tension between discretion and the formal demands of the *rule of law*. Extensive use of discretion in the application of law can threaten the principles of predictability, legality, and equal treatment. Second, there is a tension between discretion and the principles of *democratic rule*. Entrusting street-level bureaucrats with extensive discretionary powers is, by definition, almost equal to relinquishing democratic control over these final steps.

There exists, of course, a great deal of sloppy discretionary work. However, that is not our point and is not what basically makes discretion problematic from the point of view of the rule of law and democracy. The two tensions are intrinsic and cannot be removed, only ameliorated. They follow from the very nature of discretion as a judgmental and decisional activity and can appear even if one presupposes that the activity is performed in a conscientious manner.

## 1. The rule of law

According to the idea of the *Rechtsstaat*, political authorities should rule by and be subject to law. There are four central principles of the rule of law.[19] First, the enforcement of laws should be predictable. Citizens should be treated in accordance with general laws, making their legal standing – their rights and duties – possible to foresee; that is, they can form rational expectations ex ante about what legal consequences their actions will have and about the legal consequences of what may happen to them (disease, unemployment, poverty). Second, what the state does to its citizens must be warranted by valid law. Nobody should risk being punished for actions that are not illegal – *nulla poena sine lege* (no penalty without law) – and state officials should be bound by and apply the law rather than act upon whim or reasons other than legal ones. Third, equal cases should be treated equally, and unequal cases unequally. If what is factually, morally, or legally similar is treated differently, or if what is factually, morally, or legally different is treated equally, there is arbitrariness. Fourth, a principle of negative freedom that draws a distinction between the public and private spheres, that is, between questions about which the state can legitimately have an opinion and questions about which the state cannot legitimately have an opinion. There is, of course, an intense and longstanding discussion about where the borders between public and private issues are to be located, but the idea of a protected private sphere is constitutive of a *Rechtsstaat*.

The discretionary element in social rights may threaten each of these four principles. The demand for *predictability* is in tension with discretion because it is not clear in advance who has a legitimate claim or to what a right holder is actually entitled. If one cannot know that in advance, rights lose their force. Social rights are particularly vulnerable in this respect because they are dependent on state finances. Our main point is, however, that the tension with predictability is intrinsic. It is created by some of the central properties of discretionary reasoning that we have discussed: the fact that discretionary reasoning is reasoning with weak warrants and unavoidably affected by certain phenomena that create variation in judgments.

When weakly specified entitlement clauses have to be filled in by discretionary reasoning in each particular case, this may also threaten the principle of *legality*. The application of law can lead to decisions based on extra-legal factors, like private values and beliefs, hence blurring the boundaries between what is valid law and what is not, or it can even lead to the creation of law on the spot, so to speak, in each individual case. This, of course, affects not only the legality but also the democratic legitimacy of discretionary judgments and decisions, which we will address below.

The tension with the principle of *equal treatment*, or formal justice, is created by the fact that discretionary rights refer to individual needs and circumstances, which should be judged by welfare state professionals. There are two potential conflicts involved. First, there is a potential conflict between two normative contexts of discretion, which we described in the previous chapter – namely, between contexts governed by the formal principle of justice on the one hand and contexts governed by the demand for individualization on the other. The formal principle of justice demands comparative consistency, whereas treating people based on their individual needs requires considerations of a noncomparative kind. If there is a clash between normative expectations or contexts, then the important issue is which context should prevail. Discretionary rights make this into a question of judgment. The other potential conflict arises from the variation-creating properties of discretionary reasoning. Variation in judgments, reflecting a close attention to particular needs and circumstances, is, indeed, the point of allowing for discretion, but there is a distinction between legitimate and illegitimate variation. Discretionary variation is legitimate if it stays within the boundaries of the formal principle of justice – that is, when the function of discretionary reasoning is to unearth the morally and legally significant differences or similarities between individuals' life situations, which justify equal or unequal treatment. Variation is, or at least can be, illegitimate if it transgresses the boundaries of the formal principle of justice – that is, if it leads to unequal treatment in the absence of morally or legally significant differences between cases or to equal treatment in the presence of relevant differences.

Variations in judgments, such as those mentioned in the case study, emanate from the very nature of discretionary reasoning. Even fully rational exercisers of discretion, motivated purely by good reasons, can reach different conclusions on the question of who should have what when their decisions are made in accordance with the aforementioned *Rule R*. The tension between professional discretion and the principles of the rule of law is, therefore, ineradicable.

The granting of extensive discretionary powers to welfare state professionals has a tendency to blur the *distinction between the public and the private*. They must involve themselves in the lives of their clients so that they can obtain adequate information about their clients, suggest viable solutions to their problems, and follow them up in a proper manner. This may lead to outright intrusion into the private lives of others.

## 2. Democracy's black hole

The "black hole of democracy," a term coined by Rothstein (see Chapter 1), is used to describe the worries concerning what is actually happening inside discretionary spaces delegated to street-level bureaucrats. Rothstein states, "It is the sum of their actions which constitutes the public program. As to whether these actions reflect the objectives laid down by the democratically constituted organs – this must be regarded as an open question."[20] The dismal answer is that, largely, one cannot know, control, or govern what is happening in the many discretionary spaces in the welfare state. A gnawing suspicion then exists that a lot of things may happen that are not in accordance with the will of democratic political bodies, which grant or accept discretionary powers. Thus, formally delegated discretionary powers and informally amassed discretionary powers raise important issues for democratic theory.[21] Below, we shall address some of the issues raised.

One democratic worry concerns *trust*. The delegation of discretionary power to professionals is based on the following two expectations: professionals will act in accordance with their professional mandate, and they possess the knowledge that is required to carry out what they are supposed to do. The first kind of expectation is motivational; the second, epistemic. In both cases, the information is asymmetric, and the principal is largely dependent on trust in the agents.

The motivational issue arises as soon as there is a suspicion that professionals do not really work in the best interests of those whom they are supposed to serve; they only pretend to do that, serving their own self-interests instead. If professionals act like "knaves" driven by self-interest instead of "knights" driven by a desire to perform services for the public, the support for a professional trust-based model of delivery of public services loses its merit relative to other forms of organization.[22]

The epistemic issue has to do with the fact that "knowledge does not 'apply itself,'" as Talcott Parsons notes.[23] Expert knowledge is acquired through formal educational programs, but these programs can only to a certain degree – and maybe not to a particularly large degree – determine how this knowledge will be applied in actual practice. The gap between textbook knowledge and the knowledge required to solve particular problems may be difficult to bridge in some cases. Possessing the "right" knowledge is also no guarantee that the "right" action will be performed because even experts make errors. Therefore, professional certification and authorization can only to a limited degree serve as a reliable source for epistemic trust. Moreover, welfare state professionals must often carry out tasks for which they perhaps lack competence or adequate training. A case in point is the role of physicians in making decisions about disability pensions even though physicians generally lack the competence to understand labor market issues and to assess the opportunities for earning a decent income in the future.

It is an often-observed feature of expert behavior that experts overstretch their competence and are overconfident.[24] One form of overstretching occurs when professionals either pretend to have an expertise in answering not only factual and but also normative questions or transform questions about what is good or right into technical questions. The democratic worry is that the delegation of discretionary power may foster *expertocracy* within the welfare state. Moral and political issues about citizens' needs and welfare are then lifted out of the sphere of public discourse, becoming questions for experts to answer instead.[25] However, are the putative experts really experts, and, above all, can someone actually be an expert on human welfare?[26] This doubt makes a case for the participation of those who are subject to discretionary expert power and for democratic monitoring and control.

The worry about expertocracy represents yet another democratic worry, which is about the *legitimacy of decisions and actions*. When professionals with discretionary powers actually determine what should be done based on their best judgment but without much control, monitoring, and democratic government of their decisions, the worry is that the exercise of public power "does not appropriately track the interests, views, or will of the citizens."[27] Even if the process of delegation itself has been correctly conducted, the outcomes of the exercise of discretionary power – the way it affects peoples' lives – may lack democratic legitimacy.

The vignette study to which we referred showed that the personal values and attitudes of GPs play a considerable role in determining how they assess cases and make decisions. For instance, GPs who are skeptical about the disability pension system are more restrictive in their assessments than less skeptical GPs. However, GPs' personal attitudes toward the disability pension system should not play any role in their judgments on patients' eligibility to receive such pensions. There is no reason to think that this is different in other professions. It may be a greater problem in professions with more vague and contested knowledge bases than that of medicine. The problem is, however, that neither GPs nor other professionals are *authorized* to judge, decide, and act on the basis of personal, moral, and political attitudes. They are authorized to make judgments and decisions on the basis of a body of formalized knowledge acquired through formal educational programs. Their personal, moral, and political values do not belong to the authorized "package." Although physicians may strongly believe in the Protestant work ethic, they are simply not authorized to use it as a basis for their assessments regarding the eligibility of patients to receive a disability pension or to let their own Protestant work ethic influence their judgments.

The reasoning and decision-making processes of welfare state professionals are influenced not only by personal values and beliefs but also by normative standards, which are more or less shared by the members of a profession or parts of the professional community. Some examples of normative standards include different conceptions of what is normal and abnormal, what is considered a need, what constitutes legitimate public support, what is "actually" in the best interests of abused children, and what is in the best interests of pupils. By adhering to such standards, professionals take positions on politically controversial issues.

In summary, the worry about legitimacy is that values, norms, and beliefs not authorized by democratic bodies are used as premises for professional judgments and decisions affecting the lives of citizens. This problem overlaps the problem that discretion creates with regard to the principle of legality. Democratic legitimacy is achieved when judgments and decisions are pursuant to democratically enacted law.

A final democratic worry is about the risk of domination, or exposure to *arbitrary power*.[28] Professionals in charge of the allocation of welfare benefits and services have both de jure control and de facto control over goods that others need or want. If their control is of a discretionary kind – as it often is – they also have discretionary power over those who need or want access to these goods. If $A$ controls some good $X$ in which $B$ has an interest (i.e., which $B$ needs or wants), then $A$ has potential power over $B$. If $A$ has complete discretion over the disposition of $X$, then $A$ can, in principle, do with $X$ as $A$ wishes. For instance, $A$ can make all sorts of demands and threats to withhold resources in cases of noncompliance.[29] Such complete or unconstrained discretion is arbitrary power. The satisfaction of $B$'s interests in $X$ then depends on $A$'s inclinations. If $A$ is maleficent, then $B$ is in trouble. If $A$ is incompetent, then $B$ is also in trouble. This is an extreme form of discretionary power. The democratically delegated discretionary power we are talking about is constrained: it is delegated "on the condition that the agent remains answerable to a common-knowledge understanding of both the goals and aims it is meant to serve, and the means of achieving those goals and aims it is permitted to employ."[30] However, cases of complete or unconstrained discretion highlight the main issue of power connected to discretion in a democracy, namely, the risk of arbitrary exercise of power over citizens in situations where they are highly dependent clients.

## Concluding remarks

We have tried to disentangle and elucidate some aspects of two normative tensions created by the extensive delegation of discretionary powers to welfare state professionals. On the one hand, there exist tensions between discretion and the demands of the rule of law; on the other hand, there exist tensions between discretion and democratic authority. These tensions cannot be *completely* removed or eliminated in a welfare state. They are not created by the potential misuse of discretionary powers but rather are intrinsic to discretion as a space for judgment and as a type of reasoning. They arise because the delegation of discretionary powers is the delegation of the power to decide and act based on one's own best judgment, which is a task fraught with tensions and ambiguities. Possessing discretionary powers means not only to be entrusted but also to have a certain degree of autonomy. It is to be accountable, but it is accountability under conditions where it is difficult to enforce. It is to be entrusted as an expert, but there is no linear connection between knowledge and action, and the problems to be solved often transcend the domain of one's putative expertise. It is to have an official role, but it is a role that is carried out by a socialized human with one's own life history and personal experiences.

## Notes

1 Marshall (1949) and Habermas (1987, 356–61).
2 Alexy (1994, 334–35).
3 For an attempt to map processes of juridification, see Blichner and Molander (2008).
4 Campbell (1978).
5 See below, p. 49–50.
6 OECD defines activation policies as aiming "to bring more people into the effective labour force, to counteract the potentially negative effects of unemployment and related benefits on work incentives by enforcing their conditionality on active job search and participation in measures to improve employability, and to manage employment services and other labour market measures so that they effectively promote and assist the return to work" (Martin 2014, 3). In addition to Martin (2014), see Eichhorst et al. (2008) for an overview of activation schemes in Europa and the US, For a discussion of justificatory issues, see Molander and Torsvik (2015).
7 See, for example, Sainsbury (2008), van Berkel et al. (2010) and Jessen and Tufte (2014).

8 Habermas (1987, 362–64). See also his discussion of "welfare state paternalism" in Habermas (1996, chap. 9).
9 Maus (1986, 306).
10 Alexy (1994, 4.II.1.1).
11 Here we have to ignore the question of human versus citizens' rights as well as the question of rights of immigrants who are not citizens.
12 http://app.uio.no/ub/ujur/oversatte-lover/data/lov-19911213-081-eng.html.
13 http://app.uio.no/ub/ujur/oversatte-lover/data/lov-19980717-061-eng.pdf.
14 Goodin (1988, 186).
15 See note 29 in chapter 1.
16 See also the example used in Bingham (2010, 49–50).
17 Terum and Nergård (1999, 2001).
18 Huber and Shipan (2002).
19 For classical statements on the rule of law as a normative standard, see Hayek (1944), Fuller (1969) and Raz (1979). For reconsiderations, see Marmor (2004). Jeremy Waldron has recently emphasized that the legal procedures needed to match the principles of the rule of law are as central to the idea of the rule of law as the principles themselves; see Waldron (2011).
20 Rothstein (1998, 80).
21 Richardson (2002).
22 Le Grand (2003) and Le Grand (2007).
23 Parsons (1951, 348).
24 Koriat et al. (1980) and Mercier (2011).
25 Dzur (2008) and Fischer (2009).
26 On trust in experts, see Goldman (2011). For a discussion of expertise and democracy, see Holst and Molander (forthcoming).
27 Richardson (2002, 7).
28 Non-domination (not being subjected to arbitrary power) is at the center of Philip Pettit's republican theory of democracy. See Pettit (2012).
29 Goodin (1988, 198).
30 Lovett (2010, 96).

# 4 Mechanisms of accountability

We have focused on professional discretion that is exercised when members of different professions act as gatekeepers of the welfare state and make decisions, or make premises for decisions, about who is entitled to what. For many welfare rights, the eligibility criteria are vague, and discretion is necessary to determine who has a right to $X$. This may also apply to the entitlement clauses that specify to what one is entitled and when one has a right or a legitimate claim to $X$. Rights that are discretionary in one way or the other, or in both ways, give professionals a more or less extensive discretionary power. The legislator leaves it up to them to assess who is entitled to what.

To what extent the allocation of benefits and services should depend on professional judgments is a central normative question of the welfare state.[1] The argument for discretion is based on the necessity of ensuring flexibility and adaptability to individual needs and circumstances. By contrast, the argument for reducing the latitude for discretion is that discretion can be abused and can lead to arbitrariness in the treatment of people. However, eliminating discretion is simply not possible. It would require the specification of general rules for all benefits and services distributed by the welfare state in such a way that entitlement in particular cases can be a matter of subsumption. Although it is possible to make certain benefits universal and unconditional, many of them will remain more or less subject to an assessment of needs and circumstances. When it comes to services, the element of discretion is even more difficult to eliminate.

The delegation of discretionary power is based on trusting that those who hold authority have the willingness and ability to perform their tasks in an acceptable manner – and, preferably, in the best way possible. Therefore, discretion also comes with a demand for accountability; that is, individuals should be able to "account" for their judgments and decisions. This condition is again based on the assumption that discretionary judgments are not whimsies but rather justified judgments.

The demand for accountability is basically a demand for rationality or reasonableness.[2] The Latin word *ratio* (in Greek, *logos*), from which "rationality" is derived, can (like *reason* and *raison*) mean both the faculty of reason (in German, *Vernunft*) and "ground" (in German, *Grund*), where the faculty of reason is the ability to give reasons, to account for one's beliefs and actions (in Latin, *rationem reddere*; in Greek, *logon didonai*).[3] Thus, the concept of accountability is internally linked to justification, the practice of giving reasons in favor of something, and it is precisely the demand for justification, and the possibility of holding agents accountable, that distinguishes discretionary power delegated to advance certain aims from arbitrary power.[4] Expectations of accountability, so to speak, force actors with discretionary power to act on the basis of their best judgment by forcing them to anticipate reactions from others who are entitled to hold them accountable. Or, this is what is assumed. How accountability works in different settings and under different conditions has to be researched.[5]

There are certainly numerous instances where discretion is exercised sloppily, and many of these instances are probably undetected and unsanctioned. However, as we have shown, the problem goes deeper than this. Even conscientious professionals who are motivated by nothing other than good reasons are fallible, and their reasoning may contain distortions caused by, for example, the use of heuristics. Moreover, even the most ideal reasoners who cannot be accused of making a single cognitive error may come to different conclusions regarding the same case. This possibility is inherent in discretion as a form of reasoning. One might expect reasonable disagreement to occur because the form of reasoning contains some noneliminable sources of variation. Hence, there are intrinsic tensions between discretion and comparative consistency, i.e., the demands of equal treatment and reproducibility.

The existence of discretion in the welfare state raises the question of how the exercise of discretion can be held accountable. Are there mechanisms in place to ensure that discretion is exercised judiciously? It is common to distinguish between different accountability mechanisms based on their direction: mechanisms that work vertically (top to bottom, and vice versa) or horizontally (e.g., collegiality), and ones that work from outside (external control) or from within (self-regulation).[6] Based on the distinction between discretion in the structural and epistemic senses, we suggest another approach. In line with this distinction, we can differentiate between two main types of accountability mechanisms – structural and epistemic – that cut across the standard classifications, focusing on the connection between accountability and the demand for justification. Structural mechanisms restrict the scope for discretion or put restrictions on the behavior of actors with discretionary authority, whereas epistemic mechanisms place emphasis on improving the conditions for and the quality of discretionary reasoning. We outline five subtypes of each of the two types of mechanisms. Although the two lists are not exhaustive, and the boundaries between structural and epistemic mechanisms, as well as between the different subtypes, are not entirely clear, they illustrate a way of thinking about how to improve professional discretion and mitigate the tensions it creates.

However, we must first turn to the concept of discretion and its relation to justification. If the exercise of discretion is to be made accountable, the space for discretion must also be – in the words of Wilfrid Sellars – a "space of reasons."[7]

## Discretion and reason giving

As we have seen, discretion has two aspects, one structural and one epistemic. On the one hand, it refers to an area where one can choose between permitted alternatives of action on the basis of one's own judgments. On the other hand, it refers to a cognitive activity, a kind of reasoning that results in judgments about what to do under circumstances of indeterminacy. Discretionary reasoning is reasoning *with weak warrants* or rules of inference. The force of a strong warrant approaches the force of a rule of deduction in logic. A weak warrant mentions only issues that ought to be considered in the process of reasoning.

This distinction between structural and epistemic discretion is often overlooked.[8] However, from a normative point of view, the epistemic aspect is fundamental because the delegation of discretionary powers is based on the assumption that the entrusted actor is capable of making reasoned judgments and decisions. The distinction is also crucial for a discussion of the accountability of discretionary power.

To illustrate the epistemic aspect of discretion, let's return to the example of a physician who examines a patient to determine whether the patient is eligible to receive a disability pension. As we mentioned, according Norwegian social security legislation, a person is eligible to receive a disability benefit if the earning ability is permanently impaired by at least 50 percent owing to illness, injury, or defect. In passing judgment about the person's earning ability, the physician raises different types of *validity claims:*[9] the diagnosis raises a claim to truth (e.g., the patient suffers from serious arthritis); the prognosis also raises a claim to truth (i.e., more than 50 percent of the patient's future ability to earn a decent income is lost); and the legal advice raises a claim to normative rightness (i.e., the patient should be eligible to receive a disability pension). By making such claims, the physician also claims that the opinions expressed are sincere – that is, the physician's best judgment, or the judgment that the physician finds to be the most convincing. This is a claim to truthfulness or sincerity. The diagnosis, prognosis, and legal advice are all defeasible: other physicians can reach other conclusions if they reexamine the patient. Lawyers, for their part, can also draw different conclusions if they reexamine the bearing of statutes or the precedents for the case. If the patient or state authorities appeal the decisions, physicians and lawyers must be prepared to defend their judgments publicly. This view of discretion has some important consequences.

One consequence is that concepts describing what it is to practice discretion are concepts that belong to a theory of argumentation. "Best judgment" is such a concept. One judgment is better than another one if it is supported by better arguments. "This is $X$'s best judgment" does not mean "This is what $X$ likes best," but rather "This is what $X$ believes is supported by the best arguments." When someone is entrusted with discretion, good arguments are what are expected from this person even if discretionary reasoning is practiced in situations of indeterminacy.

Another consequence follows from the fact that the obligation to provide justifications is an obligation to others (e.g., delegating authorities, affected parties). This puts constraints on the kind of reasons that can be used to justify discretionary judgments, decisions, and actions. The reasons must fall within the scope of public reasons, that is, they must be generally accessible. It is, however, often explicitly said that discretionary judgments express tacit knowledge, intuition, holistic thinking, bodily sensibilities, receptiveness, and many other things. Such factors, at best, generate nonpublic reasons, that is, reasons that cannot be assessed by others. Intuition and special sensibilities may be important, but they do not per se provide the kinds of reasons that must be used to justify discretionary judgments by professionals in public roles. Professionals are granted discretionary powers on the basis of certified knowledge, and they are expected to justify their decisions by reference to this knowledge as well as to laws and generally accepted principles.

Yet another consequence is that one can make sense of why someone can be entrusted with discretionary powers. It is difficult to understand why someone ought to be entrusted with discretion if a discretionary space is only a license to do what one wants, but it is comprehensible if holders of discretionary powers incur an obligation to justify their defeasible judgments with public reasons. It is the fact that discretionary judgments raise defeasible but defensible validity claims that justifies the entrustment of such powers to officials and professionals. If $A$ has discretion over $X$, $A$ is entrusted to make decisions about $X$ based on $A$'s best judgment. This implies a demand for accountability.

## Accountability

Accountability is a threefold predicate: someone is accountable to someone else with respect to something. An agent with discretionary power is accountable *to* the principal who has bestowed trust upon the agent *for* how the responsibilities entailed in using this power are carried out.[10] In common usage, the term *accountability* is associated with the process of being called "to account" for what one does or has done.[11] The closest synonym is *answerability*, which "indicates that being accountable to somebody implies the obligation to respond to nasty questions and, vice versa, that holding somebody accountable implies the opportunity to ask uncomfortable questions."[12] To be accountable in this sense means that one may be asked not only to provide information about one's judgment, decisions, and actions, but also to *justify* them. Justifications can be good or bad, and those who can demand justifications are not entitled to bad justifications. Thus, the main characteristic of accountability is the quality of justifications; that is, the one who has a right to ask questions is entitled to receive a good answer. The currency of accountability is, so to speak, is good reasons, and the basic meaning of accountability can be stated as follows:

1   *A* is accountable to *B* if *A* has a duty to justify his or her judgments, decisions, and actions to *B*. *A*'s duty to justify his or her judgments, decisions, and actions stems from *B*'s right to demand justification.
2   Thus, *A* has a duty to justify his or her decisions, judgments, and actions to *B* because *B* has a right to demand such justification.

However, accountability cannot be understood as a purely discursive relation between the accountable and accounting parties. It implies more than the interchange of questioning and answering. "Agents must not only be 'called' to account; they must also be 'held' to account."[13] Accountability demands reactions to misconduct and failed justifications; otherwise, it deteriorates to reporting.[14] Reporting differs from accountability in another way: it does not necessarily imply argumentative justification of judgments, decisions, or actions; reports can be purely descriptive. In epistemic terms, there is thus a crucial difference between reporting and justifying judgments, decisions, and actions. There can be good reports of bad actions, for instance. The core of good reporting is to provide adequate descriptions, whereas the core of accountability is good reasoning. Accountability, according to Mark Bovens, is "a relationship between an actor and a forum, in which the actor has an obligation to explain and to justify his or her conduct, and in which the forum can pose questions and pass judgment, and the actor may face consequences."[15] Without accountability there would be no control of what is occurring in discretionary spaces. Its aim is to ensure that agents take their responsibilities seriously and act in a way that is publicly justifiable.[16]

There are different devices for making holders of discretionary power accountable. Based on our analysis of discretion, professional discretion can be made more accountable by implementing structural mechanisms targeting discretionary spaces or epistemic mechanisms targeting discretionary reasoning. The main aim of structural mechanisms is to constrain or narrow such discretionary spaces or to constrain the actions of persons who operate in discretionary spaces, whereas the main aim of epistemic mechanisms is to improve the quality of discretionary judgments by improving the reasoning process or the conditions for reasoning. The distinction is, of course, rough. Structural mechanisms are mainly a matter of control but may have epistemic side effects. Epistemic mechanisms are internally related to reason giving but may require matching structural mechanisms. A borderline case comprises review procedures. They are structural mechanisms, but they can actually put persons with discretion under a kind of pressure that will motivate them to argue better and to work in a more conscientious and thorough way. They thus have the potential to improve the quality of discretionary reasoning.

## Structural mechanisms

Structural mechanisms reduce the number of cases where persons with discretionary power can act on the basis of their own best judgment alone. In essence, such mechanisms exemplify a very simple logic: if one cannot know what occurs in a discretionary space, and if politically, morally, and legally questionable things can actually be occurring there, then one should ensure that as few things as possible are occurring there or simply remove the space, if one can. In a welfare state, this logic cannot be completely carried out without relinquishing all arrangements based on the evaluation of need and individualized treatment. However, particular discretionary spaces can be constrained or removed. Using Dworkin's doughnut metaphor, some structural measures can be said to squeeze the hole de jure by tightening the belt of restriction. Others attempt to constrain discretion even if the hole in the doughnut can be formally as big as before. They squeeze the hole de facto by restraining the actors' opportunity for moving in the hole even if the actors have the same formal autonomy as before.

Here we distinguish five main subclasses of structural mechanisms with different targets: punitive, restricting, divisive, delaying, and blocking mechanisms.

## 1. Punitive mechanisms

Punitive mechanisms target de facto behavior in discretionary spaces. The idea behind them is that credible ex ante threats will restrain possible trespassers. They involve a mix of control, monitoring, and review arrangements by which an authority (normally the authority that has granted discretionary powers) can check that the use of discretion is in accordance with rules and guidelines. Authorities can react to noncompliance or sloppy use of discretion in different ways. They can change decisions made by inferiors. They can instruct that practices in a field be changed. They can reorganize institutions and conduct random inspections. The sanctions can range from various forms of correcting mechanisms (e.g., reprimands) to fines and firings. The most dramatic of all sanctioning mechanisms, with the exception of criminal charges, is the suspension or withdrawal of delegation. A certain number of physicians, nurses, psychologists, and lawyers lose their licenses to practice each year. Some lose their licenses because of sexual misconduct, some because of drug or alcohol abuse, and some because of, for instance, their leniency in prescribing medicines to patients or because of malpractice. In some cases, their licenses are not withdrawn; instead, these individuals receive a formal reprimand and perhaps a temporary license suspension.

## 2. Restricting mechanisms

Rights and the specification of rules belong to the class of structural mechanisms. Rights constrain discretionary spaces by specifying and clarifying entitlements and obligations. When entitlements and obligations are clearly specified, rights holders have the possibility to complain, to appeal, and eventually to bring cases to court if they disagree with decisions. One effect of introducing rights and making welfare rights less discretionary is that holders of discretionary powers can be compelled to justify their judgments, decisions, and actions. Hence, rights can have epistemic effects although they belong to the class of structural mechanisms in the first place.

An increased use of rights does not in itself make discretion superfluous. In principle, clearer material rules could compensate for the discretionary element in many social rights, at least when it is possible to specify the need in question in such a way that entitlement could be considered to be a matter of subsumption. It is, however, an open issue as to how far it is possible to "tidy up" discretionary social rights, especially with regard to services. However, even in a system with well-specified entitlements, decision makers would have to relate to many situational and personal matters, which demands flexibility of judgment and decision-making. The provision of economic support and other kinds of help for disabled persons is a case in point. The same amount of money can have very different values for different persons, depending on the nature of their functional impairment and where they live. We do not mean to say that stricter entitlement rules should not be used as a structural mechanism of accountability. However, there are limits to what degree such rules can be specified, and there are good reasons for formulating the entitlements of persons in need as discretionary rights.

## 3. Divisive mechanisms

Divisive accountability mechanisms work by targeting the relationship between discretionary spaces and the holders of discretionary powers. These mechanisms are divisive in the sense that they attempt to split formerly coherent spaces held by one person among several holders of discretionary powers, thus reducing the power of each single person. In doing so, they establish systems of internal checks and balances in discretionary spaces, thereby reducing the power of each single holder of discretionary powers.

When individuals are granted discretionary powers, they are often granted a package that consists of judgments, decisions, and actions. One could split up this package and invest its different parts in different persons. The one who judges need not be the same as the one who decides, who in turn need not be the same as the one who acts. When decisions can have dramatic consequences, it may be best to separate these powers.

Such a separation of discretionary powers is exemplified by the Norwegian police force. When on street patrol, Norwegian police officers are unarmed, but they do keep firearms in a locked box in their patrol cars. They cannot unilaterally decide to use their firearms; they first have to contact their superiors. In cooperation, the street-level officers and their superiors then decide whether the street-level officers should use their firearms.[17] Such a procedure slows down the decision-making process and offers the opportunity for those involved to have second thoughts. It slows down trigger-happy officers, for instance, and gives superiors the opportunity to judge before they decide whether the use of firearms in an actual situation is within the regulations that govern police behavior. The basic reason for this procedure is to reduce the number of casualties caused by shootings. The procedure is, however, controversial. The main counterargument is that it endangers the lives of police officers and others.

## 4. Delaying mechanisms

When the separation of discretionary powers is institutionalized as a mechanism of accountability, the reasons can both be that several minds think better than one and that with regard to certain consequential decisions, it is better to have time to reflect and perhaps solicit the views of affected parties and others before the decision is made. A time delay can also allow others, for instance, concerned parties, to be involved in the decision-making process. It opens up the possibility that others have time to react and make their views and concerns known. Delaying simply extends the reaction time and opens up opportunities for action. Actually, this was one of Max Weber's points about the advantages of the collegial organization of decision-making processes. Collegiality tempers decision-making processes by slowing them down.[18] This also connects to the research on heuristics and cognitive biases. A switch to "slow" and deliberative thinking is the remedy against the pitfalls of "fast" thinking using intuitive heuristics.[19] Medical decisions are often made too fast, with many diagnostic errors resulting, under the illusion that time is more scarce than it actually is.[20] Mechanisms that slow down the processes of judging, deciding, and acting can be advantageous, for instance, from the point of view of reducing certain kinds of errors. There is every reason to assume that this is not specific to the field of medicine.

## 5. Blocking mechanisms

Blocking mechanisms target holders of discretionary powers in their capacity as office holders. These mechanisms can, for example, block reelection or reappointment and, thus, restrict the number of periods of incumbency. They can also block simultaneous incumbency in different offices, as well as impose a time delay in the transition from one office to other offices, a period of quarantine, so to speak. In addition, they can constrain the possibility of acting as a judge of the quality of one's own previous judgments. For example, the judges and juries in appeal courts are not the same as those used in courts at a lower level.

The main reason behind blocking mechanisms is to prevent the intrusion of certain kinds of vested interests into the office holder's judgments and decisions. Thus, blocking mechanisms to a certain extent address the problem of the intrusion of illegitimate private concerns into professional judgments. They also target the problem of mixed motives and mixed interests more generally. If office holders have too many offices, it may be difficult to keep them separate. If they stay too long in one office, they may develop an interest in staying there because of private benefits, power or prestige. If they are permitted to combine certain kinds of offices, for instance, a job as a hospital physician and a job as a consultant for a company producing and marketing medical products, then their private interests can gain the upper hand. Therefore, it is problematic if physicians and other professionals combine certain positions or offices.

### *Epistemic mechanisms*

The point of epistemic mechanisms is to improve the quality of discretionary reasoning by improving either the process or the conditions of reasoning. These mechanisms are directed at discretionary reasoning, not at discretionary spaces. A special kind of reactions is connected to epistemic mechanisms. They are based on the principle that those who have not reasoned adequately can or must correct their mistakes through better reasoning. They may be obliged to defend themselves for certain critical forums. They will then have to think carefully about the arguments they use to defend their decisions. If their defenses do not pass the argumentative test, they will have to change their opinions.

We distinguish five main subclasses of epistemic mechanisms with different targets: formative, supportive, motivational, deliberative, and participatory mechanisms.

*1. Formative mechanisms*

Formative mechanisms aim to inculcate specific kinds of knowledge, modes of thinking, values, and norms in persons with discretionary powers. Of the formative mechanisms, the most important is, of course, formalized educational programs, which transfer the knowledge, norms, and values that are the basis for obtaining authorization to practice as a professional. The basic idea behind an educational program seen as an accountability mechanism is that different persons with the same formal education will judge, decide, and act in a more informed, uniform, and consistent manner than those who lack a common formal education. Sharing similar formal education backgrounds is expected to raise the quality of judgments and contribute to less variability in judgments and decisions across persons. It is, of course, an empirical question of whether or not this is so.

We have drawn attention to the massive influence of heuristics with their concomitant cognitive biases on human reasoning. Research seems to suggest that neither more knowledge nor more experience is particularly efficient in itself with regard to countering the influence of heuristics. Both laypeople and experts seem to be under the influence of heuristics even if they already know about them. However, what does seem to work, in some cases at least, is teaching people to think and reflect in certain ways about how they are thinking and then explicitly and consciously to adopt counterstrategies to their cognitive biases.[21] Basically, the way to block biases emanating from the intuitive "System 1" is to learn to "recognize the signs that you are in a cognitive minefield, slow down, and ask for reinforcement from System 2," whose operations are deliberately controlled.[22] This is a typical issue of formation. Through teaching cognitive strategies, one aims at improving the quality of discretionary reasoning by forming the mindsets of persons with discretionary powers.

*2. Supportive mechanisms*

The targets of supportive mechanisms are the decision situations of persons with discretionary powers. Various kinds of decision support systems belong to this subclass. Research seems to show that when decision makers can rely on different kinds of decision support, they are liable to make fewer mistakes and to judge, decide, and act in a more consistent manner.[23] Evidence-based practice is one example.

An oft-quoted definition of evidence-based practice states the following:

> Evidence-based medicine is the conscientious, explicit, and judicious use of current best evidence in making decisions about the care of individual patients.... [It] means integrating individual clinical expertise with the best available external clinical evidence from systematic research.[24]

Although some authors use wider definitions and others use narrower definitions, these definitions have the same central idea: different kinds of knowledge can be ranked based on scientific merit, strength of evidence, or methodological quality, especially when applied to knowledge about the effects of interventions (i.e., "what works"). All defenders and practitioners of evidence-based practice operate with what can be called an evidence hierarchy. At the top of this hierarchy is evidence from studies with a randomized control trial (RCT) design or meta-analyses of studies with an RCT design. Evidence from expert committee reports or opinions and from the clinical experience of respected authorities is placed at the bottom. Essential to the approach are meta-analyses of existing studies (e.g., an examination of evidence to determine whether an intervention actually works or not).

From the evidence hierarchy follows a certain kind of decision procedure. This procedure may have more or fewer steps, but it starts with defining the problem and ends with formulating an intervention based on the most relevant and applicable findings – or what is often called the "best available evidence." The best available evidence is found if one starts searching at the top of the hierarchy and moves downward. However, there does not seem to be agreement about how evidence basing should relate to clinical judgments. Some defenders of the approach want it to enrich clinical judgments, whereas others (although rather few) see it as an alternative to or replacement for clinical judgment.

An evidence-based approach targets the decision situations of professionals and aims to supply decision makers with the most updated and reliable knowledge about which interventions work and which interventions do not work. It has spread very rapidly from medicine to many other fields, such as teaching and social work.[25] Therefore, it is important to clarify where evidence basing is suitable and where it is not suitable as a measure of accountability. Studies documenting "what works" are helpful in answering clinical questions, but it is contested as to what extent evidence-based reasoning can inform decisions about which treatment should be chosen. In fields such as education and social work, evidence is more uncertain compared with evidence in medicine, and it is true for all fields that evidence-based reasoning alone is not able to fill in if–then clauses regulating who is entitled to what.

## 3. Motivational mechanisms

Motivational mechanisms target the motivational structure or makeup of actors with discretionary powers. What distinguishes them from structural mechanisms is that they do not come in the form of external constraints on discretionary spaces or on the behavior of holders of discretionary powers. They work from the inside, so to speak. Their point is to motivate such actors to do a good job – in this case, to carry out thorough and conscientious discretionary reasoning. Such mechanisms come in different forms. Although material incentives have been the focus of principal–agent models, incentives may also take the form of recognition and trust.[26] A mechanism not based on sanctions and rewards is what Richard Thaler and Cass Sunstein call "nudging" or "choice architecture." Mutatis mutandis, we may think of "discretion architecture," that is, how one – by arranging the decision situation in a certain way – can nudge holders of discretionary power to act in a more reflective and responsible way.[27]

An important insight from the accountability point of view is that institutional arrangements can foster different types of motivation, and especially that they may foster undesired behavior. For example, studies have shown that pay for performance schemes do not work well in professional settings, such as health care and education, and may even have perverse effects.[28] The reason is the so-called multitask problem.[29] It is hard to measure "health care" and "education," and when doctors or teachers (or their hospitals or schools) are rewarded for certain targets, they may direct their attention to these targets to the detriment of tasks that are not easily quantifiable and rewarded. This may result in substandard work. The worst case is so-called gaming. In this type of situation, doctors or teachers not only conform to the target but also (some) try to make as much as possible out of the incentive scheme, even by directly misusing it.[30] How an incentive scheme works is dependent on the agents' motivations, that is, to what extent they are intrinsic or extrinsic, other-regarding or self-interested. An incentive scheme can also influence motivations. Economic incentives may crowd out intrinsic motivation and eventually turn altruistic "knights" into self-interested "knaves."[31] However, motivations are always mixed, and the designing of schemes for professional work must take this fact into account.

## 4. Deliberative mechanisms

Deliberative epistemic mechanisms target the arguments put forth by persons with discretionary powers. The point is to test the validity of arguments, either before or after decisions have been made.

Deliberation means to weigh reasons for and against something. It takes place both internally (in the heads of individuals) and externally (in collective settings).[32] In the same way, deliberative accountability mechanisms can also be of two basic types. One type tries to influence the deliberation of individual decision makers by getting them to anticipate a situation where they would have to justify their judgments and decisions. For example, a random sample of cases could regularly be selected for review in a forum, either anonymously or not. The assumption is that the mere knowledge of the possibility of being exposed to review and discussion would induce or "nudge" decision makers to reason as if they had to justify their actions to an audience.[33] The probability of being selected for review, which is required for this mechanism to work, is, however, uncertain. It is also uncertain how the anticipation of a context of justification will affect the quality of reasoning. The other type of deliberative mechanism is of an external collective kind. The aim of this mechanism is to establish *arenas* where arguments can be examined in critical discussions, progressing from arenas with narrow audiences to arenas with wide audiences. Here we explore this type of deliberative mechanism further.

A) DELIBERATIVE ARRANGEMENTS WITH NARROW AUDIENCES

One example of a discursive arena with a narrow audience is a collegial body. Collegiality is a way of reaching decisions through deliberation among peers.[34] Collegial bodies are created to examine whether conduct complies with norms and ethical codes of the profession and to bring clarity to "hard" cases. However, in these bodies, professionals are responsible only to their peers.

Court-like institutions in welfare administration are another example of a discursive arena with a narrow audience. A court-like institution possesses some of the important characteristics of a proper court, such as procedures for a fair trial, rules for the inclusion of affected parties, an autonomy vis-à-vis the administration, and the possibility of appealing decisions to higher instances.

The Norwegian National Insurance Court is an example of such a court-like body. Its area of competence is to make decisions about rights and duties in accordance with national insurance and pension legislation. It is a freestanding institution with expert knowledge that settles disputes between the Norwegian Labour and Welfare Administration and members of the national insurance system (i.e., citizens). It has precedential force, and its verdicts can be brought directly before the Court of Appeal.[35]

## Mechanisms of accountability 73

Another Norwegian example of a court-like body is the County Boards of Child Protection and Social Welfare, which handles, for example, cases where the transfer of child custody is considered, owing to abuse, lack of proper care, and so on. Normally, a board consists of three members: one moderator (a lawyer), one expert, and one layperson. The procedural rules of this body mimic the rules of civil dispute settlements, and the aim is to increase the probability of making decisions that are in the best interests of the child. Such a board can be seen as a forum in which deliberation assumes the form of advocatory discourses on behalf of the child.[36]

An ombudsman is also an example of a court-like institution. Ombudsmen cannot overturn the decisions of lower instances, but they can ask for reports and justifications for decisions. In doing so, they can stimulate the (self-) reflection of decision makers and, thus, give input that can lead to an improvement of their reasoning.

One can also imagine more purely deliberative bodies that do not decide concrete cases (or appeals) but instead discuss and try to reach a consensus about how to decide in prototypical but difficult cases. In such forums, ordinary citizens and/or representatives for affected parties or typical users can be included. By forming shared opinions about how rules and guidelines are to be understood, such forums can contribute to a more competent, consistent, and uniform practice of discretion.

B) DELIBERATION WITH WIDE AUDIENCES

An accountability relationship between those who possess discretionary powers and those who are subjected to them also requires a broader forum – the public sphere – where decision makers can be called to account. Here we arrive at the fundamental sense of accountability in a democratic *Rechtsstaat*, namely, the duty to provide justifications for judgments, decisions, and actions to citizens.

In the public sphere, welfare state professionals and institutions can be forced to relate to citizens experiences and opinions. Through public discussions, unsolved tasks can be identified and social problems can be revealed, as well as ineffective welfare programs, illegitimate paternalist practices, malpractice, and so on. Thus, the public sphere carries out important functions with regard to the setting of standards and the monitoring of discretion practiced by welfare state professionals. Measuring the effect of public debate and criticism on norms and practices is, however, difficult.

A major problem from a deliberative perspective is that the public sphere all too often fails to function in a deliberative way. Among other things, the phenomenon of mediatized politics is well known: spectacular cases effectively sponsored by commercial news interests rather than by real and serious problems catch the attention of the public. However, proponents of deliberative theory have sought to design procedures for handling the possible deficiencies of public debate. For a number of years, James S. Fishkin has been engaged in the Deliberative Polling research program, which seeks to encourage people to reconsider – rather than confirm – their views by exploring what opinions they would support if they knew more and thought more about the issues. First, a random sample responds to a survey, and then the respondents convene for many hours of deliberation, both in small groups and in plenary sessions in which they can pose questions to politicians and experts and exchange competing points of view.[37] The idea is that the outcome of deliberation in such mini-publics should represent a more "refined" public opinion. In our context, this method could be used in connection with hard cases, in the evaluation of welfare programs, and in preparation of welfare reforms.

## 5. Participatory mechanisms

The main characteristic of a participatory measure of accountability is that it includes affected and concerned parties as decision makers and not merely as discussants or as audiences. Participatory mechanisms widen the group or class of decision makers, so to speak. Extended participation is an element in many of the deliberative mechanisms we have previously discussed. They include not only professionals as colleagues but also affected and concerned parties. However, these parties and the public are mainly included as discussants and as audiences. So the question is, are there epistemic accountability mechanisms that include affected parties as decision makers? And if there are, what would be the point of such mechanisms? What would they target, and what would they yield from the point of view of accountability and discretion?

An obvious candidate would be different procedures for *co-decision*. These procedures specify which concerned or affected parties must participate in the decision-making process before a decision is valid. They specify who has decision-making powers in a certain kind of case. The most prominent examples of co-decision procedures are found in two-chamber parliaments, where some proposals must be accepted in both chambers so as to be valid. Procedures in professional contexts, which are strongly reminiscent of co-decision procedures, are suggested by some of the participants in the longstanding discussions about adequate models of the relations between health care staff and patients.[38] Basically, they suggest that health care staff should make decisions about treatment regimes in cooperation with their patients. There are parallel proposals for client participation in frontline decision-making with regard to social benefits and services.[39]

A main function of co-decision procedures as seen from the point of view of accountability is that they de facto introduce a demand for mutual justification into the interaction between the co-decision makers. If the co-decision makers must agree for a decision to be valid, they must convince, so to speak, one another of the validity of the proposed decision; otherwise, there will be no decision. So it is imaginable, at least, that well-designed co-decision procedures can contribute to improving the quality of discretionary reasoning simply by introducing a demand for mutual justification into a decision-making procedure. The different parties participating in the procedure must then review and discuss one another's justification to find out whether these justifications are acceptable or not. As part of this process, the parties involved may refine their arguments or change their preferences. An obvious problem is, however, that the relationship is asymmetrical. On the one hand, professionals may use their position to persuade their patients or clients by latent strategic communication instead of communication aimed at achieving mutual understanding. On the other hand, participatory procedures may bring false beliefs and bad arguments into the dialogue.

## Concluding remarks

Imagining the welfare state without the delegation of discretionary power to professionals is difficult to the extent that benefits and services are allocated based on assessments of needs. Even if rules could be thoroughly specified, gatekeepers must take a variety of situations and personal circumstances into account, which requires flexibility and, thus, the exercise of discretion. At the same time, the delegation of discretionary power leads to difficult "accountability" issues. When one approaches these problems, it is helpful to consider the proposed distinction between discretion in the structural sense and discretion in the epistemic sense. One must also consider both aspects of discretion when suggesting ways in which the exercise of discretion can be made accountable. The mechanisms outlined here demonstrate how this can be done. However, accountability is no panacea. How different mechanisms will work and the extent to which they can actually improve the quality of discretionary reasoning is a matter for empirical research.

## Notes

1. Goodin (1988, chap. 7).
2. According to Adam Smith (1776/1976, 111), accountability is also constitutive of morality: "A moral being is an accountable being," who "must give an account of its actions to some other." This passage was, however, deleted in the last (sixth) edition of Smith's *Theory of Moral Sentiments*. See Darwall (2006).
3. Tugendhat (1975, 107).
4. Lovett (2010, 96).
5. Tetlock (1992, 337), Lerner and Tetlock (1999).
6. See, for example, Mulgan (2003, 26 ff).
7. Sellars (1997, 76).
8. This is, for example, the case with Goodin's seminal analysis of discretion in the welfare state. It is, as we have seen, based on the "limiting case" of "complete" discretion, which, according to Goodin, means "that that person is not obliged to have, much less to give, any reasons whatsoever for deciding one way rather than another" (Goodin 1988, 198).
9. On validity claims, see Habermas (1984, 8–42).
10. Dunn (1999).
11. Mulgan (2000, 555). See also Mulgan (2003, chap. 1).
12. Schedler (1999).
13. Mulgan (2003, 9).
14. Schedler (1999, 16).
15. Bovens (2007). See also Bovens et al. (2014).
16. Cf. Norman Daniels on "accountability for reasonableness" (e.g. Daniels 2008, chap. 4) with regard to priority setting in health care.
17. Thanks to Tatanya Ducran Valland for her help with this example.
18. Weber (1978, 273).
19. Kahneman (2011).
20. Groopman (2007).
21. Groopman (2007).
22. Kahneman (2011, 417).
23. Kirkebøen (2009).
24. Sackett et al. (1996).
25. Hansen and Rieper (2009).
26. Brennan and Pettit (2004) and Ellingsen and Johannesson (2007).
27. Thaler and Sunstein (2008). We use nudges here in a different way than Thaler and Sunstein. They are concerned with how individuals' choices related to health and welfare can be improved. The nudges they suggest make use of cognitive biases so as to nudge people in a direction of choices that make them "better off." They call this "libertarian paternalism." The nudges thought of here do not track cognitive biases; they instead nudge actors to improve their reasoning.
28. Lemière et al. (2013).
29. Holmstrom and Milgrom (1991).
30. In Norway, hospitals are partly financed by fixed amounts of money allotted by the state according to diagnoses or diagnostic-related groups. Some diagnoses are expensive and bring in a great deal of money. Other diagnoses are not so costly and bring in less money. So the temptation is great to report many more expensive diagnoses than have actually been set, simply because that brings in more money to the hospital. This was exactly what was done in one hospital.

Somebody "upgraded" diagnoses from one price class to higher price classes so as to obtain more money from the state.
31 Le Grand (2003).
32 Goodin (2003).
33 Compare the reasoning in Torsvik et al. (2011). As we have already mentioned, such review procedures exemplify that there is no clear-cut border between structural and epistemic mechanisms. The possibility of being exposed to review is basically a structural measure, but it may have epistemic effects. Here the intention of the procedure is to promote internal deliberation.
34 Parsons (1978) and Sciulli (1992).
35 Kjønstad and Syse (2005, 90).
36 Eriksen and Skivenes (2001).
37 Fishkin (2009).
38 Emanuel and Emanuel (1992).
39 Handler (1986) and Handler (1992).

# 5 Summing up

The aims of this little book are threefold: (a) to gain a better insight into the phenomenon of discretion, (b) to explain why the extensive delegation of discretionary powers to different professional groups in the welfare state is problematic, and (c) to outline what can be done about it. These three aims are connected. A better idea of what can be done requires a better understanding of why the delegation of discretionary powers is problematic, which in turn requires a better insight into the practice of discretion.

We suggest a conceptualization of discretion based on a distinction between discretionary space and discretionary reasoning or between discretion in a structural and in an epistemic sense. In a structural sense, discretion consists of permissible courses of action and constitutes the discretionary power of agents who are entrusted to act on behalf of somebody, or in someone's best interest. In the epistemic sense, discretion designates the cognitive activity performed within such spaces, that is, reasoning under conditions of indeterminacy.

We claim that the extensive delegation of discretionary powers is problematic for two main reasons: there exist intrinsic tensions between discretion and justice and between discretion and democracy. The former type of tension is between discretion and the formal demands of the rule of law. Tensions of this type concern arbitrariness, capriciousness of law enforcement and policy implementation, uncertainties about what is actually valid law, and illegitimate intrusions in the private lives of citizens. These tensions evoke a series of worries about unfair treatment and the legal certainty of citizens.

The latter type of tension concerns democratic monitoring, control, and government. These tensions evoke a series of worries about what persons with discretionary powers are actually doing – the claim being that much of what they are doing is outside democratic control but can have dramatic consequences for people's lives. Persons with discretionary powers may overstretch their competences, create expertocracies, and implement laws and policy programs in ways that may contradict the intentions of democratically elected legislators and policymakers. They may shape welfare states at the street level, without proper democratic control.

We consider the tensions between discretion, justice, and democracy to be unavoidable in principle. Welfare states cannot do without discretion as long as welfare benefits and services are distributed based on need and entitlement to such benefits and services is couched in more or less discretionary social rights.

However, measures can be carried out to ease these tensions and make the judgments, decisions, and actions of holders of discretionary powers more accountable. We outline a series of accountability measures in light of the conceptual apparatus introduced in this book. The main distinction is between structural and epistemic mechanisms. The point of the former is to constrain discretionary spaces or the behavior within them, whereas the point of the latter is to improve the quality of discretionary reasoning.

# Bibliography

Abbott, Andrew (1988). *The System of Professions: An Essay on the Division of Expert Labor*. Chicago: University of Chicago Press.
Adler, Michael, and Stewart Asquith (eds.) (1981). *Discretion and Welfare*. London: Heinemann Educational Books.
Alexy, Robert (1983). *Theorie der juristischen Argumentation*. Frankfurt am Main: Suhrkamp.
Alexy, Robert (1994). *Theorie der Grundrechte*. Frankfurt am Main: Suhrkamp.
Alexy, Robert (2002). *Afterword to a Theory of Fundamental Rights*. Oxford: Oxford University Press.
Aristotle (1976). *Ethics*. Translated by J.A.K. Thomson. Revised with notes and appendices by Hugg Tredennick. London: Penguin Books.
Arrow, Kenneth J. (1963). "Uncertainty and the Welfare Economics of Medical Care." *American Economic Review* 53, no. 5: 939–973.
Barak, Aharon (1989). *Judicial Discretion*. New Haven, CT: Yale University Press.
Baumgartner, M.P. (1992). "The Myth of Discretion." In *The Uses of Discretion*, edited by Keith Hawkins. Oxford: Clarendon Press.
Berlin, Isaiah (1969). "Two Concepts of Liberty." In *Four Essays on Liberty*. Oxford: Oxford University Press.
Bingham, Tom (2010). *The Rule of Law*. London: Allen Lane.
Blichner, Lars, and Anders Molander (2008). "Mapping Juridification." *European Law Journal* 14, no. 1: 36–54.
Bovens, Mark (2007). "Analysing and Assessing Accountability: A Conceptual Framework." *European Law Journal* 13, no. 4: 447–468.
Bovens, Mark, Thomas Schillemans, and Robert Goodin (2014). "Public Accountability." In *The Oxford Handbook of Public Accountability*. Oxford: Oxford University Press.
Brennan, Geoffrey, and Philip Pettit (2004). *The Economy of Esteem: An Essay on Civil and Political Society*. Oxford: Oxford University Press.
Brodkin, Evelyn Z. (1997). "Inside the Welfare Contract: Discretion and Accountability in State Welfare Administration." *Social Service Review* 71, no. 1: 1–33.
Brodkin, Evelyn Z. (2013). "Street-Level Organizations and the Welfare State." In *Work and the Welfare State: Street-Level Organizations and Workfare Politics*, edited by Evelyn Z. Brodkin and Gregory Marston. Washington, DC: Georgetown University Press.

Buchanan, Allen (1988). "Principal/Agent Theory and Decision Making in Health Care." *Bioethics* 2, no. 1: 317–333.
Buchanan, Allen (1996). "Towards a Theory of the Ethics of Bureaucratic Organisations." *Business Ethics Quarterly* 6, no. 4: 419–440.
Campbell, Tom (1978). "Discretionary Rights." In *Philosophy in Social Work*, edited by N. Timms and D. Watson. London: Routledge and Kegan Paul.
Cicero (1991). *On Duties*. Edited by M.T. Griffin and E.M Atkins. Cambridge: Cambridge University Press.
Coleman, Jules L., and Brian Leiter (1993–1994). "Determinacy, Objectivity, and Authority." *University of Pennsylvania Law Review* 142.
Connolly, Terry, Hal R. Arkes, and Kenneth R. Hammond (eds.) (1999). *Judgment and Decision Making*, 2nd ed. Cambridge: Cambridge University Press.
Croskerry, Pat (2005). "The Theory and Practice of Clinical Decision-Making." *Canadian Journal of Anesthesia* 52, suppl. 1: R1–R8.
Daniels, Norman (2008a). "How Can We Meet Health Needs Fairly When We Can't Meet Them All? Accountability for Reasonable Resource Allocation." In *Just Health*, edited by Norman Daniels. Cambridge: Cambridge University Press.
Daniels, Norman (2008b). *Just Health: Meeting Needs Fairly*. Cambridge: Cambridge University Press.
Darwall, Stephen (2006). *The Second-Person Standpoint*. Cambridge, MA: Harvard University Press.
Davis, Kenneth C. (1969). *Discretionary Justice: A Preliminary Inquiry*. Baton Rouge: Louisiana State University Press.
Dicey, A.V. (1885/1915). *Introduction to the Study of the Law of the Constitution*, 8th ed. London: Macmillan. Reprint 1988, Indianapolis, IN: Liberty Classics.
Dunn, Delmer D. (1999). "Mixing Elected and Nonelected Officials in Democratic Policy Making: Fundamentals of Accountability and Responsibility." In *Democracy, Accountability, and Representation*, edited by Adam Przeworski, Susan C. Stokes, and Bernard Manin. Cambridge: Cambridge University Press.
Dworkin, Ronald (1977). *Taking Rights Seriously*. Cambridge, MA: Harvard University Press.
Dzur, Albert W. (2008). *Democratic Professionalism: Citizen Participation and the Reconstruction of Professional Ethics, Identity and Practice*. University Park, PA: Pennsylvania State University Press.
Eddy, David M. (1982). "Probabilistic Reasoning in Clinical Medicine: Problems and Opportunities." In *Judgment under uncertainty: Heuristics and Biases*, edited by D. Kahneman, P. Slovic, and A. Tversky. Cambridge: Cambridge University Press.
Eichhorst, Werner, Otto Kaufmann, and Regina Konle-Seidl (eds.) (2008). *Bringing Jobless People into Work: Experiences with Activation Schemes in Europe and the US*. Heidelberg: Springer.
Ellingsen, Tore, and Johannesson, Magnus (2007). "Paying Respect." *Journal of Economic Perspectives* 21, no. 4: 135–150.
Emanuel, Ezekiel J., and Linda L. Emanuel (1992). "Four Models of the Physician–Patient Relationship." *Journal of the American Medical Association* 267, no. 16: 2221–2226.
Eriksen, Andreas (2015). "The Authority of Professional Roles." *Journal of Social Philosophy* 46, issue 3.

# Bibliography

Eriksen, Erik Oddvar, and Marit Skivenes (2001). "Legitimeringsproblemer i Barnevernet?" In *Demokratiets sorte hull – om spenningen mellom fag og politikk i velferdsstaten*, edited by E.O. Eriksen. Oslo: Abstrakt forlag.

Feinberg, Joel (1974). "Noncomparative Justice." *Philosophical Review* 83, no. 3: 297–338.

Feldman, Martha (1992). "Social Limits to Discretion". In *The Uses of Discretion*. Edited by Keith Hawkins. Oxford: Oxford University Press.

Fischer, Frank (2009). *Democracy and Expertise: Reorienting Policy Inquiry*. Oxford: Oxford University Press.

Fishkin, James S. (2009). *When the People Speak: Deliberative Democracy and Public Consultation*. Oxford: Oxford University Press.

Freidman, Milton (1962). *Capitalism and Freedom*. Chicago: University of Chicago Press.

Freidson, Eliot (2001). *Professionalism: The Third Logic*. Cambridge: Polity Press.

Fuller, Lon L. (1969). "Threshold of Procedural Norms." In *The Morality of Law*. New Haven, CT and London: Yale University Press.

Galligan, D.J. (1986). *Discretionary Powers: A Legal Study of Official Discretion*. Oxford: Clarendon Press.

Gauthier, David P. (1963). *Practical Reasoning*. Oxford: Clarendon Press.

Gilovich, Thomas, Dale Griffin, and Daniel Kahneman (eds.) (2002). *Heuristics and Biases: The Psychology of Intuitive Judgment*. Cambridge: Cambridge University Press.

Girgenzer, Gerd (2004). "Fast and Frugal Heuristics: The Tools of Bounded Rationality." In *The Blackwell Handbook of Judgment & Decision Making*, edited by D.J. Koehler and N. Harvey. Oxford: Blackwell Publishing.

Goldman, Alvin (2011). "Experts: Which Ones Should You Trust?" In *Social Epistemology: Essential Readings*, edited by A. Goldman and D. Whitcomb. Oxford: Oxford University Press.

Goodin, Robert E. (1988). *Reasons for Welfare: The Political Theory of the Welfare State*. Princeton, NJ: Princeton University Press.

Goodin, Robert E. (2003). *Reflexive Democracy*. Oxford: Oxford University Press.

Groopman, Jerome (2007). *How Doctors Think*. Boston, MA and New York: Houghton Mifflin.

Günther, Klaus (1988). *Der Sinn für Angemessenheit*. Frankfurt am Main: Suhrkamp.

Günther, Klaus (2008). "Liberale und diskurstheoretische Deutungen der Menschenrechte." In *Rechtsphilosophie im 21. Jahrhundert*, edited by Winfired Brugger, Ulfrid Neumann, and Stephan Kirste. Frankfurt am Main: Suhrkamp.

Habermas, Jürgen (1984). *The Theory of Communicative Action*. Vol. 1, *Reason and the Rationalization of Society*. Translated by Thomas McCarthy. Boston, MA: Beacon Press.

Habermas, Jürgen (1987). *The Theory of Communicative Action*. Vol. 2, Lifeworld and System: A Critique of Functionalist Reason. Translated by Thomas McCarthy. Boston, MA: Beacon Press.

Habermas, Jürgen (1994). "On the Pragmatic, the Ethical and the Moral Employments of Practical Reason." In *Justification and Application*. Cambridge, MA: MIT Press.

Habermas, Jürgen (1996). *Between Facts and Norms: Contributions to a Discourse Theory of Law*. Translated by William Rehg. Cambridge, MA: MIT Press.

Handler, Joel F. (1986). *The Conditions of Discretion: Autonomy, Community, Bureaucracy*. New York: Russell Sage Foundation.

——— (1992). "Discretion: Power, Quiescence, and Trust." In *The Uses of Discretion*, edited by Keith Hawkins. Oxford: Oxford University Press.

Hansen, Hanne Foss, and Olaf Rieper (2009). "The Evidence Movement: The Development and Consequences of Methodologies in Review Practices." *Evaluation* 15, no. 2: 141–163.

Hart, H.L.A. (1961). *The Concept of Law*. Reprinted with corrections 1972. Oxford: Clarendon Press.

Hawkins, Keith (1992). "The Use of Legal Discretion: Perspectives from Law and Social Science." In *The Uses of Discretion*, edited by Keith Hawkins. Oxford: Clarendon Press.

Hayek, Friedrich A. (1944). *The Road to Serfdom*. London: Routledge.

——— (1960). *The Constitution of Liberty*. Chicago: University of Chicago Press.

Heath, Joseph (2014). *Morality, Competition and the Firm*. Oxford: Oxford University Press.

Hempel, Carl G. (1970). "Aspects of Scientific Explanation." In *Aspects of Scientific Explanation and Other Essays in the Philosophy of Science*. New York: Free Press.

Hill, Michael (2005). *The Policy Process*, 4th ed. Harlow: Pearson Longman.

Hobbes, Thomas (1979). *Leviathan*. Introduction by K.R. Minogue. Everyman's Library. London: J.M. Dent.

Höffe, Otfried (2001). *Königliche Völker. Zu Kants kosmopolitischer Rechts- und Friedenstheorie*. Frankfurt am Main: Suhrkamp.

Holmstrom, Bengt, and Paul Milgrom (1991). "Multitask Principal-Agent Analyses: Incentive Contracts, Asset Ownership, and Job Design." *Journal of Law, Economics, & Organization* 7, special issue: 24–52.

Holst, Cathrine, and Anders Molander (forthcoming). "Accountability of Experts." *Social Epistemology*.

Huber, John D., and Charles R. Shipan (2002). *Deliberate Discretion: The Institutional Foundations of Bureaucratic Autonomy*. Cambridge: Cambridge University Press.

Hupe, Peter, Michael Hill, and Aurélien Buffat (eds.) (2015). *Understanding Street-Level Bureaucracy*. Bristol: Policy Press.

Jamous, H., and B. Peloille (1970). "Professions: Or Self-Perpetuating Systems? Changes in the French University-Hospital System." In *Professions and Professionalization*, edited by J.A. Jackson. Cambridge: Cambridge University Press.

Jessen, Jorunn Theresia, and Per Arne Tufte (2014). "Discretionary Decision-Making in a Changing Context of Activation Policies and Welfare Reforms." *Journal of Social Policy* 43, no. 2: 269–288.

Jowell, Jeffrey (1973). "The Legal Control of Administrative Discretion." *Public Law* 18: 178–220.

Kahneman, Daniel (2011). *Thinking Fast and Slow*. New York: Farrar, Straus and Giroux.

Kahneman, Daniel, and Amos Tversky (1974). "Judgment under Uncertainty: Heuristics and Biases." *Science* 185, no. 4157: 1124–1131. Reprinted in "Judgment and Decision Making," 2d ed., *Cambridge Series on Judgment and Decision Making*, edited by Terry Connolly, Hal R. Arkes, and Kenneth R. Hammond, 35–52. Cambridge: Cambridge University Press, 1999.

Kant, I. (1785/1997). *Foundations of the Metaphysics of Morals*. Translated with an introduction by Lewis White Beck, 2nd ed., Revised. Upper Saddle River, NJ: Prentice-Hall International.

Kant, I. (1781/1965). *Critique of Pure Reason*. Translated by Norman Kemp Smith. New York: MacMillan, St. Martins Press.

Kant, I. (1991). *Political Writings*. Edited by H.S. Reiss. 2nd enlarged ed. Cambridge: Cambridge University Press.

Keren, Gideon, and Karl Halvor Teigen (2009). "Yet Another Look at the Heuristics and Biases Approach." In *Blackwell Handbook of Judgment & Decision Making*, edited by Derek J. Koehler and Nigel Harvey. Oxford: Blackwell.

Kirkebøen, Geir (2009). "Decision Behaviour – Improving Expert Judgement." In *Making Essential Choices with Scant Information: Front-End Decision Making in Major Projects*, edited by Terry M. Williams, Knut Samset, and Kjell J. Sunnevåg, 169–194. New York: Palgrave Macmillan.

Kjønstad, Asbjørn, and Aslak Syse (2005). *Velferdsrett*, 3rd ed. Oslo: Gyldendal Akademisk.

Koller, Peter (1997). *Theorie des Rechts*, 2nd and enlarged ed. Wien: Böhlau-Studienbücher.

Koriat, A., Lichtenstein, S., and Fischhoff, B. (1980). "Reasons for Confidence." *Journal of Experimental Psychology: Human Learning & Memory* 6: 107–118.

Larson, M.S. (1977). *The Rise of Professionalism: A Sociological Analysis*. Berkeley, CA and Los Angeles, CA: University of California Press.

Le Grand, Julian (2003). *Motivation, Agency, and Public Policy: Of Knights and Knaves, Pawns and Queens*. Oxford: Oxford University Press.

Le Grand, Julian (2007). *The Other Invisible Hand*. Princeton, NJ: Princeton University Press.

Lemière, C., C.H. Herbst, G. Torsvik, O. Mæstad, K. Soucat, and K.L. Leonard (2013). *Evaluating the Effects of Result-Based Financing (RBF) Schemes on Health Workers' Performance*. Draft report. Washington: World Bank.

Lerner, J.S., and P.E. Tetlock (1999). "Accounting for the Effects of Accountability." *Psychological Bulletin*, 125(2): 255–75.

Lévi-Strauss, Claude (1966). *The Savage Mind*. Chicago: University of Chicago Press.

Lipsky, Michael (1980). *Street-Level Bureaucracy: Dilemmas of the Individual in Public Services*. New York: Russell Sage Foundation.

Lovett, Frank (2010). *A General Theory of Justice and Domination*. Oxford: Oxford University Press.

Macdonald, Keith M. (1995). *The Sociology of the Professions*. London: Sage Publications.

Marmor, Andrei (2004). "The Rule of Law and Its Limits." *Law and Philosophy* 23, no. 1: 1–43.

Marshall, T.H. (1949). *Citizenship and Social Class*. The Marshall Lectures, Cambridge University. Cambridge: Cambridge University Press. Reprinted in Marshall, T.H. and Bottomore, T, *Citizenship and Social Class*. London: Pluto Press, 1992.
Martin, John P. (2014). "Activation and Active Labour Market Policies in OECD Countries: Stylized Facts and Evidence on their Effectiveness." *IZA Policy Papers* No. 84.
Mashaw, Jerry L. (1983). *Bureaucratic Justice*. New Haven, CT and London: Yale University Press.
Maus, Ingeborg (1986). "Verrechtlichung, Entrechtlichung und der Funktionswandel von Institutionen." In *Rechtstheorie und politische Theorie im Industrikapitalismus*. München.
Meehl, Paul E. (1954). *Clinical versus Statistical Prediction: A Theoretical Analysis and a Review of the Evidence*. Minneapolis, MN: University of Minnesota Press.
Mercier, Hugo (2011). "When Experts Argue: Explaining the Best and the Worst of Reasoning." *Argumentation* 25: 313–327.
Meyers, Marcia K., and Susan Vorsanger (2003). "Street-Level Bureaucrats and the Implementation of Public Policy." In *Handbook of Public Administration*, edited by B. Guy Peters and Jon Pierre. London: Sage.
Miller, Seumas (2010). *The Moral Foundations of Social Institutions: A Philosophical Study*. Cambridge: Cambridge University Press.
Molander, Anders, and Gaute Torsvik (2015). "Getting People into Work: What (If Anything) Can Justify Mandatory Activation of Welfare Recipients?" *Journal of Applied Philosophy* 32, no. 3.
Montesquieu (1949). *The Spirit of Laws*. Translated by Thomas Nugent. With an introduction by Franz Neumann. New York: Hafner Press.
Mulgan, Richard (2000). "'Accountability': An Ever-Expanding Concept?" *Public Administration* 78, no. 3: 555–573.
Mulgan, Richard (2003). *Holding Power to Account: Accountability in Modern Democracies*. Houndmills: Palgrave MacMillan
O'Neill, Onora (1996). *Towards Justice and Virtue: A Constructive Account of Practical Reasoning*. Cambridge: Cambridge University Press.
Parsons, Talcott (1951). *The Social System*. London: Routledge and Kegan Paul.
Parsons, Talcott (1978). "Research with Human Subjects and the 'Professional Complex.'" In *Action Theory and the Human Condition*. New York: Free Press.
Pettit, Philip (2012). *On the People's Terms: A Republican Theory and Model of Democracy*. Cambridge: Cambridge University Press.
Polanyi, Michael (1958). *Personal Knowledge*. London: Routledge and Kegan Paul, 1973.
Pufendorf, Samuel (1673/1991). *On the Duty of Man and Citizen*. Edited by Bu James Tully. Cambridge: Cambridge University Press.
Ramsøy, Natalie R. and Lise Kjølsrød (1986). "Velferdsstatens yrker." In *Det Norske samfunn*, edited by L. Allden, N.R. Ramsøy, and M. Vaa. Oslo: Gyldendal Norsk forlag.
Rawls, John (1955/1999). "Two Concepts of Rules." In John Rawls, *Collected Papers*. Edited by Samuel Freeman. Cambridge, MA: Harvard University Press.

Rawls, John (1971). *A Theory of Justice*. Cambridge, MA: Belknap Press of Harvard University Press.
Rawls, John (1993). *Political Liberalism*. New York: Columbia University Press.
Raz, Joseph (1979). *The Authority of Law*. Oxford: Oxford University Press.
Richardson, Henry S. (2002). *Democratic Autonomy: Public Reasoning about the Ends of Policy*. Oxford: Oxford University Press.
Rothstein, Bo (1998). *Just Institutions Matter: The Moral and Political Logic of the Universal Welfare State*. Cambridge: Cambridge University Press.
Sackett, David L., William M.C. Rosenberg, J.A. Muir-Gray, R. Brian Haynes, and W. Scott Richardson. (1996). "Evidence Based Medicine: What It Is and What It Isn't." *British Medical Journal* 312: 71–72.
Sainsbury, Roy (2008). "Administrative Justice, Discretion and the Welfare to Work Project." *Journal of Social Welfare & Family Law* 30, no. 4.
Schedler, Andreas (1999). "Conceptualizing Accountability." In *The Self-Restraining State: Power and Accountability in New Democracies*, edited by Andreas Schedler, Larry Diamond, and Marc F. Platter. London: Lynne Rienner Publishers.
Scheuerman, Bill (1994). "The Rule of Law and the Welfare State: Toward a New Synthesis." *Politics & Society* 22, no. 2: 195–213.
Schneider, Carl. E (1992). "Discretion and Rules: A Lawyer's View". In *The Uses of Discretion*. Edited by Keith Hawkins. Oxford: Oxford University Press.
Sciulli, David (1992). *Theory of Societal Constitutionalism: Foundations of a Non-Marxist Critical Theory*, ASA Rose Monograph Series. New York: Cambridge University Press.
Sciulli, David (2009). *Professions in Civil Society and the State*. Leiden and Boston, MA: Brill.
Sedulsky, Richard, and Daniel Sedulsky (2015). *The Future of Professions*. Oxford: Oxford University Press.
Sellars, Wilfred (1997). *Empiricism and the Philosophy of Mind*. Cambridge, MA: Harvard University Press.
Shapiro, Susan (1987). "The Social Control of Impersonal Trust." *American Journal of Sociology* 93, no. 3: 623–658.
Shapiro, Susan (2005). "Agency Theory." *Annual Review of Sociology* 31: 263–284.
Sharma, Anurag (1997). "Professional Agent: Knowledge Asymmetry in Agency Exchange." *The Academy of Management Review* 22, no. 3: 758–798.
Simon, Herbert A. (1957). *Models of Man.* New York: John Wiley and Sons, Inc.
Smith, Adam (1759/1976). *The Theory of Moral Sentiments*. Edited by D.D. Raphael and A.L. Macfie. Oxford: Clarendon Press. Reprint, Liberty Fund, Inc., Indianapolis, 1982.
Smith, Adam (1776/1979). *An Inquiry into the Nature and the Causes of the Wealth of Nations: Wealth of Nations*. Edited by D.D. Raphael and A.L. Macfie. Oxford: Clarendon Press. Reprint, Liberty Fund, Inc., Indianapolis, 1981.
Solum, Lawrence (2010). "Indeterminacy." In *A Companion to Philosophy of Law and Legal Theory*, edited by Dennis Peterson. Cambridge: Blackwells.
Sunstein, Cass R. (1993). "On Analogical Reasoning." *Harvard Law Review* 106, no. 3: 741–791.

Bibliography 87

Taylor, Charles (1986). "What's Wrong with Negative Liberty?" In *Philosophy and the Human Sciences: Philosophical Papers 2*. Cambridge: Cambridge University Press.

Terum, Lars Inge and Trude B. Nergård (1999). "Medisinsk skjønn og rettstryggleik." *Tidsskrift for Den norske lægeforening* 119, no. 15: 2192–2196.

Terum, Lars Inge and Trude B. Nergård (2001). "Uførepensjon og likebehandling." In *Virker velferdsstaten?* edited by A.H. Bay, B. Hvinden, and C. Koren. Oslo: Høyskoleforlaget.

Tetlock, Philip E. (1992). "The Impact of Accountability on Judgment and Choice: Toward a Social Contingency Model." *Advances in Experimental Social Psychology* 25.

Thaler, Richard H., and Cass R. Sunstein (2008). *Nudge: Improving Decisions about Health, Wealth, and Happiness*. New Haven, CT: Yale University Press.

Titmuss, Richard M. (1971). "Welfare 'Rights,' Law and Discretion." *Political Quarterly* 42, no. 2: 113–132.

Torsvik, Gaute, Anders Molander, Sigve Tjøtta, and Therese Kobbeltvedt (2011). "Anticipated Discussion and Cooperation in a Social Dilemma." *Rationality and Society* 23, no. 2: 199–216.

Toulmin, Stephen E. (1958). *The Uses of Argument*. Cambridge: Cambridge University Press.

Tugendhat, Ernst (1975). *Vorlesungen zur Einführung in die sprachanalytische Philosophie*. Frankfurt am Main: Surhkamp.

van Berkel, Rik, Paul van der Aa, and Nicollete van Gestel (2010). "Professionals without a Profession? Redesigning Case Management in Dutch Local Welfare Agencies." *European Journal of Social Work* 13, no. 4: 447–463.

Vinzant, Janet C., and Lane Crothers (1998). *Street-Level Leadership: Discretion & Legitimacy in Frontline Public Service*. Washington, DC: Georgetown University Press.

Waldron, Jeremy (2011). "The Rule of Law and the Importance of Procedure." In *Getting to the Rule of Law: NOMOS L*, edited by James E. Fleming. New York: New York University Press.

Wallander, Lisa, and Anders Molander (2014). "Disentangling Discretion: A Conceptual and Methodological Approach." *Professions and Professionalism* 4, no. 3.

Wallander, Lisa, and Anders Molander (2016). "Learning to Reason: The Factorial Survey as a Teaching Tool in Social Work Education." *Nordic Social Work Research*. Published online, 04 June.

Weber, Max (1978). *Economy and Society*. Edited by Guenther Roth and Claus Wittich. Berkeley, CA: University of California Press.

Wellmer, Albrecht (1993). "Freiheitsmodelle in der modernen Welt." In *Endspiele: Die unversöhnliche Moderne*. Frankfurt am Main: Suhrkamp.

Wittgenstein, Ludwig (1953). *Philosophical Investigations*. Oxford: Basil Blackwell.

# Index

Abbott, A. 3, 6
accountability 4–5, 22–4, 60–75
accountability mechanisms 5, 65–75; epistemic 5, 68–74; structural 5, 65–8
Alexy, R. 10, 58–9
arbitrariness / arbitrary power 3–4, 13–15, 35, 53, 57–8, 59, 60–1
Aristotle 10–11, 18, 39, 46
Arrow, K.J. 6
autonomy 9–10, 23–4, 58, 65

Barak, A. 9
bounded rationality 12, 17
burdens of discretion 4, 25, 37–41

Cicero 11, 18
circumstances of discretion 25, 28–30, 41
collegiality 5, 61, 67, 72
comparative consistency 32–8, 40–1, 45, 54, 61
competence 24, 56, 78
contexts of discretion 25, 31–6, 54

Davis, K.C. 6, 9, 18
decision support 69–70
deliberation / deliberative 68–9, 72–5
democracy / democratic 4–5, 16–17, 47–8, 51–9, 78–9
Dicey, A.V. 13, 18
discretion: epistemic 4, 61–2; structural 4, 61–2
discretionary power 2–5, 9, 13–16, 20, 24, 47, 52–3, 55–8, 60–75, 78–9
discretionary reasoning 4, 10, 20–4
discretionary rights 50, 54, 66

discretionary space 4, 10, 20–4
distributive justice 48
domination 3, 57, 59
Dworkin, R. 10, 18, 20–1, 46, 65

Eddy, D. 42
education 24, 56, 57, 69
entrustment 3–4, 21–4, 63–4
equal treatment 5, 29, 32–5, 54–5, 61
evidenced-based practice (medicine) 70–1

fairness 11, 33–4, 36
formal justice 29, 32, 35, 54

Galligan, D.J. 9, 18
Goodin, R. 9, 13–15, 18, 51, 59, 75–6

Habermas, J. 46, 47–8, 58
Hayek, F. von 13, 18, 59
heuristics 4, 17, 28, 36, 41–5, 61, 68–9
Hobbes, T. 7, 9–10

incentives 71
indeterminacy 3–4, 10, 25, 28, 38–9, 62–3, 78
individualization 8, 12, 32–5, 54

Jowell, J. 9, 18
juridification 47
justification 2, 21–3, 26, 32–3, 37, 46, 63–4. 66, 72

Kahneman, D. 19, 42–4, 46
Kant, I. 11–12, 18

motivation 70–1

negative freedom / liberty 9, 21, 23, 53
noncomparative justice 35

Parsons, T. 6, 56, 59, 77
Polanyi, M 39, 46
principal–agent 2, 16, 71
professions 1–5
public reasons 4, 63
Pufendorf, S. 11

Rawls, J. 46, 47–8, 58
reasonable disagreement 4, 37, 46, 61
*Rechtsstaat* 47–8, 53–4, 73
reproducibility 32–5, 61
review 65, 72, 75, 76–7
rights 48–51
Rothstein, B. 18–19, 55, 59
rule of law 29, 48, 53–5, 58–9, 78

Simon, H. 17
Smith, A. 1, 6, 75
social rights (welfare rights) 5, 47–51, 54, 60, 66, 79
street-level bureaucrats 2, 4–5, 16, 32, 50, 53, 55, 67, 79
Sunstein, C.R. 46, 71, 76

Titmuss, R.M. 12. 18
Toulmin, S.E. 25–6, 42
trust 1, 55–6, 59–60
Tversky, A. 42–4, 46

validity claims 62, 76

warrants 25–45, 54, 62
Weber, M. 18, 67, 76
welfare state 1–3, 5, 9, 13, 16, 27, 34, 45, 47–59, 60–2, 65, 73, 75, 76, 78–9; professionals 3, 13, 52, 54, 58, 73
Wittgenstein, L. 11, 18

# Taylor & Francis eBooks

## Helping you to choose the right eBooks for your Library

Add Routledge titles to your library's digital collection today. Taylor and Francis ebooks contains over 50,000 titles in the Humanities, Social Sciences, Behavioural Sciences, Built Environment and Law.

Choose from a range of subject packages or create your own!

**Benefits for you**
- Free MARC records
- COUNTER-compliant usage statistics
- Flexible purchase and pricing options
- All titles DRM-free.

**Benefits for your user**
- Off-site, anytime access via Athens or referring URL
- Print or copy pages or chapters
- Full content search
- Bookmark, highlight and annotate text
- Access to thousands of pages of quality research at the click of a button.

REQUEST YOUR FREE INSTITUTIONAL TRIAL TODAY

**Free Trials Available**
We offer free trials to qualifying academic, corporate and government customers.

## eCollections – Choose from over 30 subject eCollections, including:

| | |
|---|---|
| Archaeology | Language Learning |
| Architecture | Law |
| Asian Studies | Literature |
| Business & Management | Media & Communication |
| Classical Studies | Middle East Studies |
| Construction | Music |
| Creative & Media Arts | Philosophy |
| Criminology & Criminal Justice | Planning |
| Economics | Politics |
| Education | Psychology & Mental Health |
| Energy | Religion |
| Engineering | Security |
| English Language & Linguistics | Social Work |
| Environment & Sustainability | Sociology |
| Geography | Sport |
| Health Studies | Theatre & Performance |
| History | Tourism, Hospitality & Events |

For more information, pricing enquiries or to order a free trial, please contact your local sales team:
www.tandfebooks.com/page/sales

 The home of Routledge books

www.tandfebooks.com